BEER, L....

& BREXIT

Our 12 month journey around Europe & North Africa

by

Andy Mckettrick

A big thank you for all the support

and encouragement during the writing of this book.

A special thanks to Mike from Holmanmedia.net for his help with the cover

"This is not a guide book. It's just a story of a couple and their dog travelling through Europe, described in a raw, honest way that only a Northerner could. Guaranteed to offend a few!"

2023 Edition.

'More Beer, more Baba, less Brexit'

Table of Contents

Chapter 1. Banter.

Chapter 2. Maintenance.

Chapter 3. Terrorists.

Chapter 4. France in the rain.

Chapter 5. Needed a miracle so we stopped at Lourdes.

Chapter 6. Hotter than a Berber's underpants.

Chapter 7. Get your pumps out, missus.

Chapter 8. Look at those little houses 'n' sh*t!

Chapter 9. Cockney in Castellon.

Chapter 10. Little bits of carrots everywhere.

Chapter 11. I've got the wife an artificial leg.

Chapter 12. Eating on an empty stomach gets you pissed.

Chapter 13. Where's all the camels, like?

Chapter 14. Forks sellotaped to twigs.

Chapter 15. This three wives idea is a nightmare.

Chapter 16. Mohammed, 2 pancakes in my gob, please.

Chapter 17. We love the French...NOT.

Chapter 18. Spanish lesson for Brexiteers part 1.

Chapter 19. The tenants.

Chapter 20. Icicles melt when you hold them.

Chapter 21. Propane is hard to light because of the dew.

Chapter 22. Every woman should have a Titbag.

Chapter 23. Walking in Elvis's footsteps.

Chapter 24. I thought I'd slip one out without you noticing.

Chapter 25. Motorhome aires, campsites and places to park.

About the Author

Andy Mckettrick is the Amazon N°.1 Bestselling author of 'Flip Flops & Falafel' – A handy guide to visiting Morocco in a Motorhome' and also 'Go West – A handy guide to visiting northern Spain in a Motorhome'.

He was born within sight of The Shankly Gates, Liverpool and after a decade as a Joiner, nine miserable years as a Driving Instructor and 'way too long' running a B&B in North Wales, he relocated to Cantabria in Northern Spain.

Other Books By Andy Mckettrick

Flip-Flops & Falafel – A handy guide to visiting Morocco in a motorhome

Go West – A handy guide to visiting Northern Spain in a motorhome

A Very Handy Travel Logbook – Motorhome, Campervan & Caravan Travel Journal

The Godfather 3

The Clangers

Bozo, Krusty & Boris

Coronation Street – Behind the glamour

Flip Flops & Falafel

Fabulous!
Thoroughly enjoyed this book. Lighthearted, informative and fun. Can't wait to get travelling again and look forward to visiting Morocco and the places Andy recommends.

Morocco, here I come!
What a lovely, insightful book. I am now looking forward to visiting Morocco. On my kindle as a reference guide for when I get there.

Funny and informative.
Lots of excellent tips and laugh-out loud funny!
Allayed any worries we had about motorhoming in Morocco and has left us really looking forward to visiting.

Cracking read!
Great entertaining read with lots of good tips and tales.
A very useful guide to visiting interesting areas of Morocco in a motorhome. Brexiteers and Daily Mail readers get a good kicking, too. Thoroughly recommended!

A must read handy guide to Morocco for an adventure yet to be taken.
We have had Morocco on our hit list of places to visit in our motorhome for quite some time. Until this book, the thought was daunting and slightly scary. Andy not only puts the unknown into simple and effective advice, he also applies it with such matter of fact in his writing that it tempts you to not only visit the country but fully experience all it has to offer and more.

If you have a motorhome and want to travel to Morocco then this book is a must.
Full of useful information. Well written, with a comical twist.

Go West

Love this book!
Andy has really whetted our appetite to explore this part of Spain. He knows his stuff as he lives in the region and travels in his motorhome throughout Northern Spain. Andy writes really well and is very funny. More importantly it contains loads of useful information and tips. Highly recommend both this and his Morocco book!

Tremendous read!
Having lived in Spain but only occasionally visited the North West on business, I was knocked out by this book. Great observations and recipes (trying Fabada tomorrow!) and tips - the best one about the vacuum cleaning (Noted and will be used Ha Ha). If you weren't thinking of visiting the North West, read this, you will.

A must have book for true Spain.
I purchased this book because like most, the only bit of Northern Spain we usually see is driving through to get to southern Spain. My husband doesn't usually read many books but this one he couldn't put down. It's great for recommendations of places to stay, the surrounding area and tips on where and what to eat. However, what gripped my husband was the humour it brings with it. We now can't wait to start discovering the places Andy recommends.

Motorhoming in Spain, an essential book.
If you are travelling to northern Spain in a motorhome this book is an essential read. Andy really knows his stuff and this book is packed with information about places to visit, where to park your van and where to eat etc. The information is presented in a light hearted, humorous way. The Costa Verde is now at the top of our "must visit" list.

Chapter 1. Banter

It was suggested by Brexit Phil, an old friend of ours, that I leave any mention of politics out of this book. To be fair, he had a point. This is not a book about politics, I don't do politics anymore but it IS a book about travelling; travelling for over a year throughout Europe without any border controls or need for passports and visas.

First of all, this is not a guide book. My plan is simply to record our journey, the good times, the bad times and probably the odd disaster. I'll give tips on where to visit, where not to visit and now and then throw in a joke at the expense of the people that voted to remove our right to make this journey. The very same people who are quite happy to drive across from Portugal to Spain as many times as they please, without any checks or questions, but do NOT want the Spanish, for example, to have the same rights or freedom when entering the UK.

So, if you admire Donald Trump, Nigel Farage and Boris Johnson and you're so thick that when you're abroad you think that everyone else is foreign apart from you, then maybe, give this book a miss.

Anyway, enough of the serious stuff.

I hope you enjoy this book.

Cheers

Andy

Chapter 2. Maintenance

Christ, where do I start?

As we are only days away from starting the main twelve month leg of our journey, I thought I'd better get around to some van maintenance. She's getting on a bit now, our Bessie. Fifteen, next month.

New mosquito door blinds fitted. Metal, this time. Gordi Baba proof! Cracks in the shower cubicle fixed. It's amazing what you can do with an old Tupperware and some Sikaflex! Next, T-Cut the whole van then waxed it. Nice and shiny!

I laid the new vinyl flooring. Nine hours on my hands and knees. Agony. Ibuprofen to the rescue! The van looks the part though. It should last another 12 months!

Every week, the missus breaks something different. If she never went in it, it would be like new!

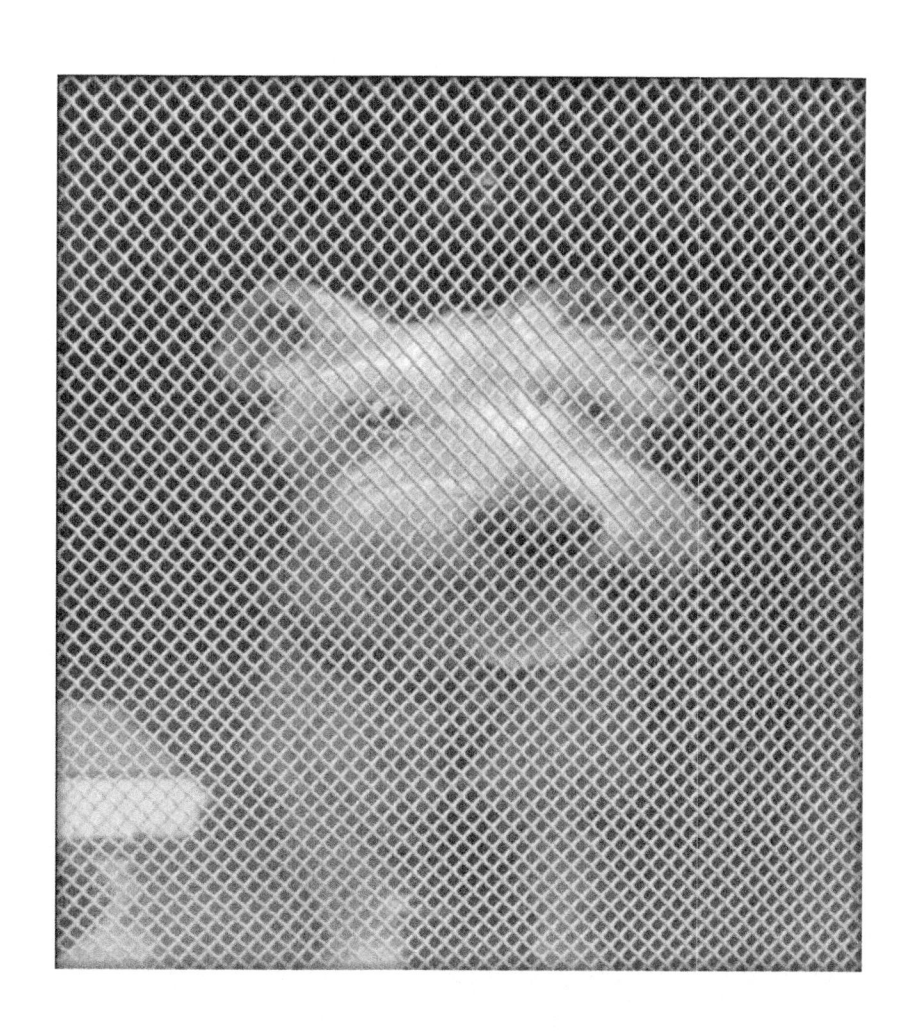

Now try and escape, you little git!

Whilst giving the van a good clean, I noticed a small drip coming from the elbow joint to the hot water heater. As you do, I decided to take it to bits. I drained the boiler, unscrewed the joint and yes, you guessed it, gallons of water started squirting out from under the sofa. Aha! I had an idea. Finger on the end of the pipe, I thought.

It was a good plan except that the nearest big towel was 3ft away and my right leg measures exactly 2ft, 11.

Tenants in the house, van dry and we're off to France.
It's a lovely place but don't go unless you've either...

A) Sold your house   B) Won the Lottery

We're off. Tesco's for diesel.

"We're off, we're off, we're off in our momo car. Fifty cops are after us and we don't know where we are"

Chapter 3. Terrorists

Down to Dover for the ferry to Dunkerque. Through France to Spain. Some time with our best mates, Pip & Karen, Castellon for Christmas then over to Morocco for three months before Germany, Switzerland, Czech Republic, Holland, Luxembourg, Belgium and wherever we pass on the way. It's a plan. It's a great plan, I reckon!

We got off the ferry in France and unloaded the terrorists from the wardrobe. Well, we could have!

Great Britain 2023. They only care about who comes **INTO** the UK. During the last 4 years there have been half a dozen homegrown terrorist attacks on UK soil and not one person in authority checks who's leaving the country! At Dover no-one asked us how many people were travelling with us. Not one person checked inside the van at all. They couldn't care less who leaves the UK. A quick glance at our passports and we were on the boat. It's a disgrace.

"You can shoot, stab and run people down all over London and you're free to leave. No problem. Just do it somewhere else next time, please."

In contrast, at Dunkerque, last time we crossed to the UK, French soldiers twice came into the van checking all the cupboards, shower cubicle etc...to check who was leaving France!

Anyway...

Off the ferry, first stop St Omer. Nothing special. Good motorhome aire, though. A decent one-nighter, at most.

Our plan is to head south following the prettiest villages in France route, using the great app Park4night as our guide. Next, straight down to Montreuil sur mer. Gorgeous place to visit. Handy free motorhome parking only 100 yards from the main town square. Next stop Ville d'Eu. Nice village. Lots of grand chateaus and stuff.

I turned around and the missus was running down the street laughing. "Stop" I said. "You don't have to steal them. They're free". She shuffled back, all sheepish. After explaining that these boxes were to place your old books in and take one that you fancy, she was quite embarrassed.

'Tea leaf'

Walked around for a few hours exploring the place. Really pretty. Recommended. I've over 1000km to do this week, so three hours driving per day, at least. Roads are brilliant. Empty and free. Not a single traffic cone. Bliss.

Visited Sanguinet, St Savinien, St Jean de Angely, Souzay Champigny, Bauge and Candes St Martin. All well worth a visit!

The lake at Sanguinet.

Stopped the night at Montreuil Bellay. Another lovely town. Free motorhome parking and services, as usual in France.

We came across a house that had human bones in the wall; left over from a stew, apparently. It's given me an idea on how to get rid of the wife. Big pan of lentils on the go if she doesn't behave!

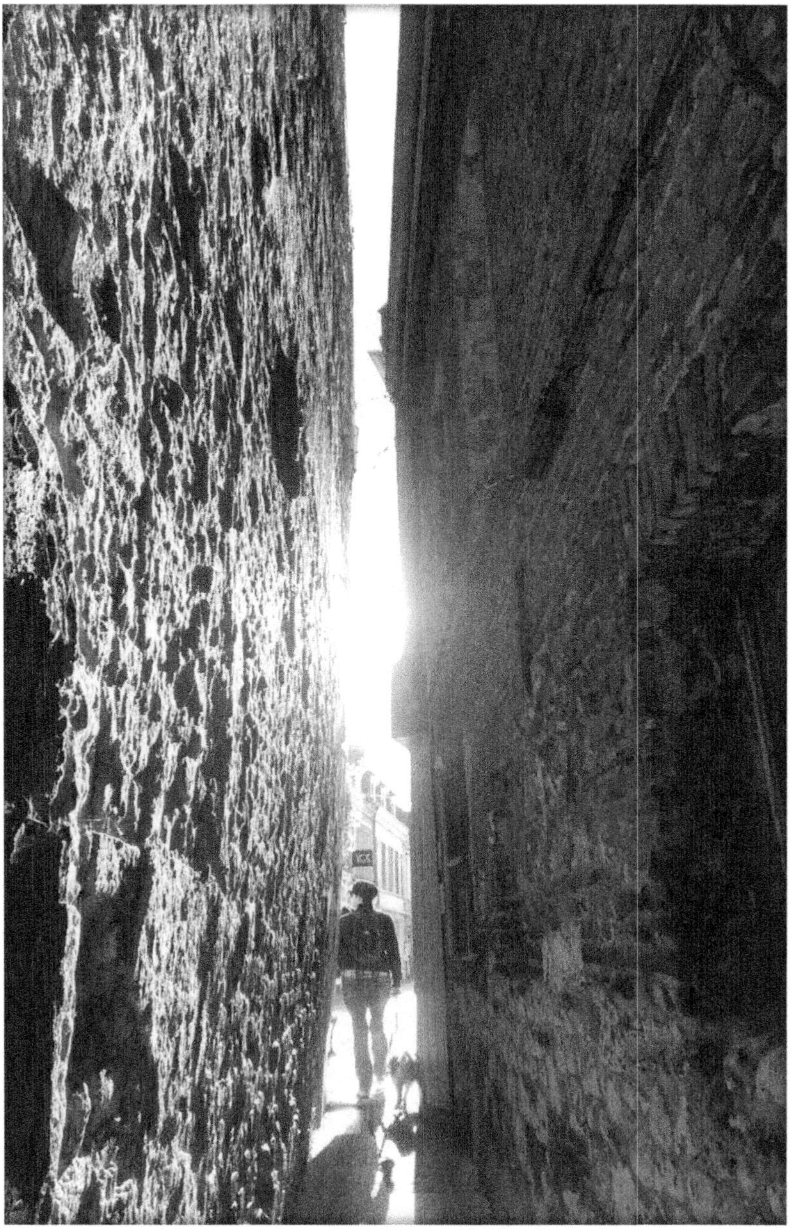

Passed through Les Lapidiales. Amazing. Like an Indiana Jones set but real.

Not paid a penny to sleep anywhere yet and no bleeding height barriers!

Kms walked 63. Pasties eaten 0. Beers demolished 11.

Chapter 4. France in the rain

"Andy. Quick!" the missus shouted.

I threw my shorts on as fast as I could. Package in. Vest on. Ran outside but it was gone. I'd missed it!

You can't really say the words 'sun' and 'France' in the same sentence. At least we are saving money on suntan lotion and at 4.80€ a coffee we need to save as much as possible!

What I love about the French is that they are very eager to please. I asked a French shop assistant "Can you charge me 3€ for that 1€ Ice lolly?" "No problem" she said. ☺

Off to Vouvant today. Really historic place. River runs right around and through the centre of the village. Stunning!

Vouvant

Gorgeous but where are all the people? It's totally dead on a Monday lunchtime. The friendly bird in the tourist office said that everything is closed on a Monday because they work Tuesday to Saturday! Makes sense?

Next village along was Pouzauges. Closed also! Apparently they've chosen Monday and Tuesday to close because they work Wednesday to Sunday!!!

It's a weird place, France. We're visiting all these gorgeous villages and they're totally empty, like museums and at 10pm everyone's tucked up in bed! I have a theory that France has a population of ten people and they get shuffled around the country every now and then so somebody can be seen. Sometimes as you enter a village, it feels like the scene from The Magnificent Seven, no people and the odd curtain twitch!

Good free parking for the night, though, right on the lake. Great sleep.

Drum roll...I found a pasty. A French, chicken pasty!

Disgusting! Horrible. Don't bother. Ever!

Ste Suzanne next. What a place. Millions of flowers.

Voted 3rd most beautiful place in France. I can see why!

We spent 3 nights there. Could have easily stayed a week! Full of 16th century half-timbered cottages with watermills and a few little cafes!

So beautiful! A MUST VISIT.

One of the many watermills in Ste Suzanne

Kms walked 42. Pasties 0. Beers 17.

Chapter 5. Needed a miracle so we stopped at Lourdes

I knew it was going to be a sh*t day when the missus woke up with one of those things that puts her in a bad mood........a pulse!

It seems that I'm banned from Facebook for a month.

Apparently somebody complained about my content and language. I broke community rules or whatever. Whoever they are, they should get a life!

I have a suggestion. Why not go outside their front door and speak to somebody not white. But I have a feeling they won't!

If they don't like what I write then don't read it, simple.

I believe that if you're not living in a way that upsets just as many people as it inspires, you're not truly living.
Living an adventurous, authentic life will piss off some and inspire others. And, sometimes it'll be hard to tell the two apart. I just follow my heart!

Toulouse.

'The rain in Spain falls mainly on the........France.
I've said it before and I'll say it again. What is the problem with France? It's always raining! It doesn't matter when we visit, June, July, August; it's more like Manchester in January!

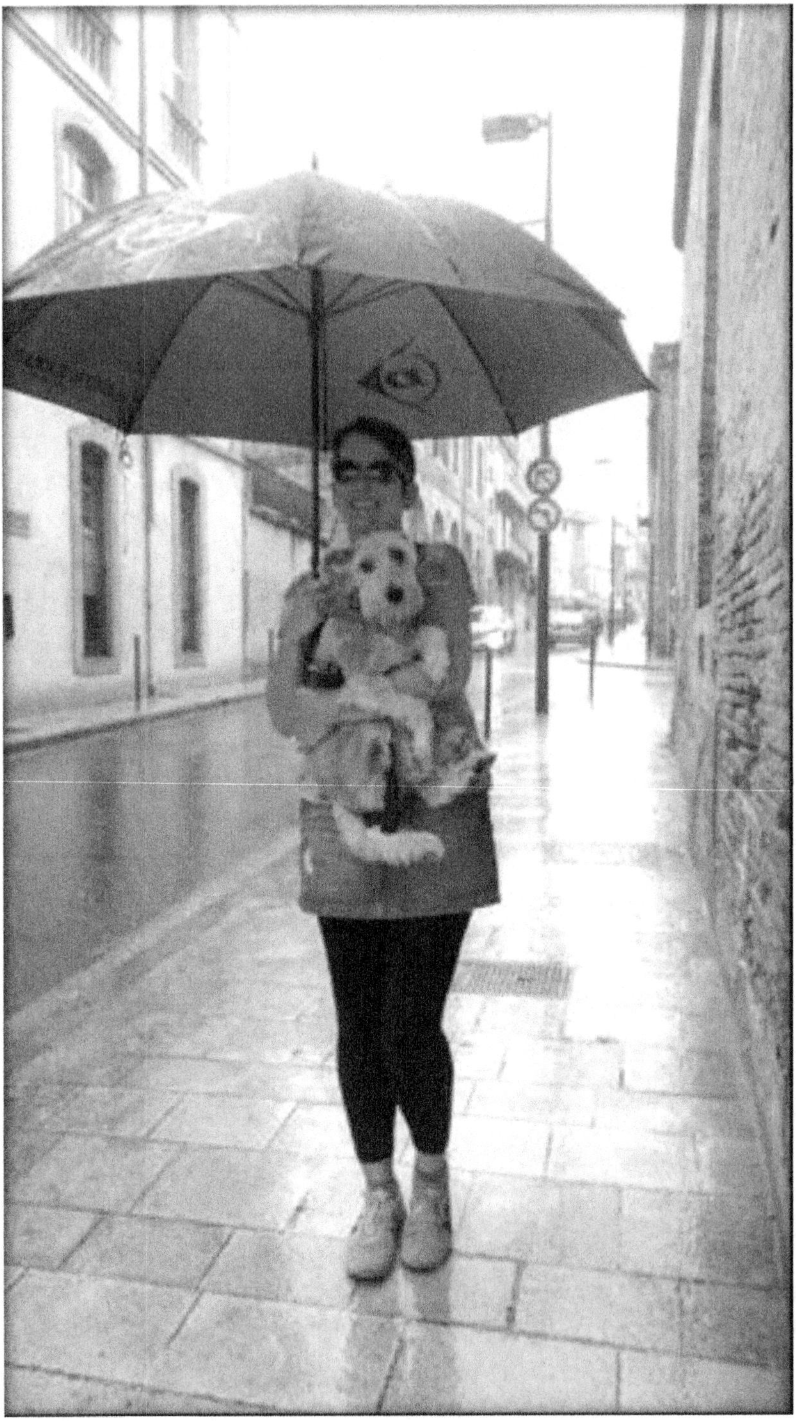

We stopped at Gaillac, Castellnau de Montmiral and Puycelsi then onto Najac for the night. All brilliant. Great free aire with free electric in Gaillac. Exactly how it should be. A town hall that welcomes visitors. One that wants us to stay for three days, all hooked up and nada to pay. We'll leave towards Lourdes, in about...err... 71hrs, then!

J.C - Area Darts Champion Nazareth 24AD

Stopped off at Lourdes in the hope that swigging some of that Holy water might help with the Champions League final tonight and the sore that I've had inside my right nostril for the last month.

Apparently, the Virgin Mary kept visiting this little cave in France and one day told a little, poor girl called Bernie to stop playing with her hula hoop and build her a massive cathedral above the cave.

"No problem", Bernie thought as she skipped all the way home. "I'm 7 years old. I can do that"

Obviously, she told her parents, who told the church, who told the family to move into a massive eight bedroom house down the road. All freebies and years before the days of housing benefit!

It must be true. No-one had any reason to lie!

We'll guess what? Liverpool lost 3 -1 and my nose is still killing me. It's all bollocks, I reckon. Elton John has stiffer wrists than our goalie. The worst use of gloves since the OJ Simpson trial.

Update - Liverpool have since won the Champions League ☺ Six times now!

Me & H

Passed through the French Basque country.

St Jean Pie de port, Ainoha and Espelette were especially pretty. We love the Basque country. Tasty food and amazing wine!

Tip : In Espelette, buy some handmade chocolates from Chocolaterie Antton. Unbelievable!

We decided to stop for the night at San Sebastian, an impressive city, to sort out my nearly new, broken, prescription sunglasses.

"I've only worn them twice and the arms fell off" I complained.

"But you've had them 6 months" the optician replied.

"Well, we've been away travelling and I emailed you months ago, multiple times and you didn't reply" I said.

"Forward me one of those emails then and I'll give you a new pair for free" he said, rather too smugly for my liking.

So, off I trotted back to the van, turned back the date on the laptop six months, wrote the email, saved it then put the date back to normal and forwarded it to him in the shop.

Sorted. Free replacement glasses. No more money from me, smartarse! ☺

Anyway, San Sebastian is an amazing place to visit. In my opinion, it's probably the most beautiful city in Spain. The old quarter has more Michelin star restaurants than anywhere else in the world (outside of Paris).

Chapter 6. Hotter than a Berber's underpants

So, the plan was to travel around Cantabria, Castilla y Leon and the Palencia region. Following the Roman ruins, bridges and old churches etc... Maybe walk a bit of the Camino de Santiago. Good exercise, I reckon!

Wake up, breakfast, coffee, shower then a three hour walk before lunch. Eat something tasty then another two or three hour walk to burn it all off. That's the secret to having a body like Brad Pitt!

Anyone that knows me knows that I'm not at all religious but I'm not travelling alone and the missus likes to visit the odd church. (She's in the Catholic cult).

Just too many unanswered questions for me. Why would God spend seven days creating the earth and everything on it and then waste a few hours to create wasps, mosquitos and parasites that eat kids eyeballs? Plus, if our creator is always watching over us then where is he when his priests are twiddling with kids bums?

If he exists, he's a kn*bhead. A leukemia inventing kn*bhead. Plus where did Noah get 2 kangaroos from, eh? eh?

Don't get me started on religion! Rant over!

~

We're not getting very far as it's just too hot. Over 34° everyday. It's unbearable in the van. Some air conditioning would be nice!

Visited Puentedey. Impressive but again, way too hot. Struggling to walk in this heat. "GIMME WATER OR BEER OR TWO BEERS, EVEN"

Tip for women - Y'know those viewing platforms that hang out over extremely high cliffs, normally made of iron grate? Well, walking sticks go right through them!

I'll give you a clue. It wasn't me!

Next, on to Cervera de Pisuerga. The town Fiestas. The usual 2 days of fake Spanish Morris dancing, fireworks etc...

I had the best tortilla de patata I've tasted in my life at bar El Patio in the main Square. A slice of tortilla, a chunk of baguette and a nice cold beer. Only 2 Euros. Life just doesn't get much better ☺

Great atmosphere but listen…we know there are fiestas in the town. There are posters for miles on every wall and shop window. Dozens of birds dolled up in the middle of the day. The usual Basque looking, wonky fringed, twentysomethings sitting in squares, drinking at 10am.

We know, OK! It's the same 2 days every year!

'Fancy dancing'

They do NOT need to spend 3 hours firing off the loudest, crappiest fireworks they've picked up from the local Chino shop.

We had to carry poor Gordi all round the town. He went and hid in the Hermitage and wouldn't come out. Sitting there shaking like a nutter. The poor, little sod.

Our next sleep was a lovely spot overlooking El Rio Pisuerga. Again, stupidly hot. Struggling. Castilla y Leon in August! It's 36° at 11am! I've had enough of this heat. Executive decision made. We need to head to the coast.

Stress.

Women! Argh! She's gone and snapped the kitchen tap off. Like 80 euros for a new one.

She's dangerous! We should call her dangerous. In fact, we're calling her 'Dangerous'.

Have you noticed that when women break something in the van "It was old and was about to break anyway"?

If anyone ever tells you that getting married was the happiest day of their lives, they are liars, obviously, and they've never found two quid down the side of the sofa!

Kms walked 84. Pasties eaten 0. Beers drank 14.

Chapter 7. Get your pumps out, missus

"Can we go to Porto?" she asked, staring at her mobile.

"Err...that's Portugal. It's like a nine hour drive away" I moaned.

"But it looks nice" she said, flashing her eyelids at me.

Portugal.

Vila Nova de Cerviera. One of our favourite Portugese towns. Halfway up the mountain, we realised that flip flops were a bad idea!

Tip: Mountain walk = Shoes.

A very difficult two hour trek later, we arrived at the top and discovered a small lake, so Gordi was in there like a shot. Covered head to toe in crap and guess what happened when we got back down…yes, the water pump packed in. Right in the middle of washing him!

A few minutes on Google, a Portugese caravan shop plus 99€ euros later and Gordi's all clean and cuddly again!

Back in the town, alongside the river, they started setting up a huge stage for a concert. "Nice one", I thought. We could go on the razz, I could put my best vest on, have a dance, get a bit squiffy and eat lots of crisps.

NOT! 10pm - 1am. Classical music. Arghhh. A hundred posh, Portugese kids attempting to play the violin. Never again. So, into the town for a few vinos, a bit of cheese and port then a bit of Fawlty towers in the van. "Don't mention the war".

Over 16,000 steps done. Bed. Struggling to sleep. Strange, annoying cough starting.

Chapter 8. "Look at those little houses 'n' sh*t"

Today's plan; get up early and visit Ponte De Lima, the oldest town in Portugal and then on to Guimarães, the birthplace of Portugal.

We had the usual super cheap coffees (0.80€) before buying the compulsory twenty litres of vino. (only 20€)

Another five hours of walking around in over 30°. Up to the castle, down from the castle. I can feel the ounces falling off me!

Enough. I'm melting "Let's go and sleep near the coast" I complained.

Tip: Don't attempt to drive in Portugal at 6pm. They're all maniacs. I've seen better drivers on scooters, in Morocco, carrying sheep!

I'm determined to learn to play the guitar this year. I've been staring at it for over 25 years. Just never found the time.

"Can't you play something else? It's enough to make me vomit". She's so supportive, the missus!

Porto.

The most beautiful city we've visited in over 14 years of travelling in our Bessie.

After a scary few minutes screaming at the GPS, we eventually parked up alongside the river Douro, the wrong side! Nevermind, it's only a two hour stroll to the centre.

What a place! If you've never been, you have to visit.

A weekend or whatever.

Porto. Just do it!

Gustave Eiffel designed one of the bridges over the Douro: the Maria Pia Bridge. Actually, it was Gustave Eiffel's last project before his famous Eiffel Tower.

Tip: The metro in Porto takes you to the beach. You can reach the coastal city of Matosinhos in less than half an hour from Trindade station. It's worth it!

Not a huge place. The old town is walkable.

Drank ever so slightly, too many beers, so we're sleeping here ☺ Over 18km walked in 34°. Knackered.

More Fawlty towers. O'reilly the builder. Bed.
Tomorrow, Vila do Conde to rest for a day or two.

Chapter 9. Cockney in Castellon

Back over to Spain. Benicarlo, Castellon. Plenty of free places to park. Amazing beaches and lots of good restaurants if you fancy eating out.

"I need more electric. You can never have too much electric. I'll get a cheap solar panel online", I thought.

A few days later it arrived and I'm jumping up and down like a idiot. "Free leccy, wehe!" Then I opened the box. WTF. No wires ☹ I'm no expert but I'm guessing they don't work without cables!

I also ordered two new leisure batteries for the girls over the phone. I forgot to talk cockney. Silly me!

Remember, Spaniards will never understand you unless you put on a cockney accent.

"2 Power Sun batteries" I said.

"Que?" he responded.

"Power sun, you have the brand 'Power Sun' batteries?" I repeated.

"Que?"

"Err…. Pawwerrr San. DOS BATTERIAS PAWERRR SAN" I screamed in my best cockney accent.

"Si, no problem Señor, Pawer San, we have in stock". ☺

~

I'm picking up the missus from Benicarlo railway station tonight, after her latest trip back to the UK. Arrives 10pm.

So, it's 9pm and I'm checking the scooter straps. All secure but no rear lights on the van? I'll park next to street light and check them, I thought. Clever!

Out I go in the 90mph gale force wind, Philips screwdriver in hand, removed the light covers and….nothing. "Obviously, it must be the fuses".

Just as I was putting the screws back in the light covers, the street light goes off! To me, this alone proves that there's no such thing as God. I can just about stand up. I can't even see the bleedin' screws and her train's due in less than 20 mins! Argh. P.S. I'm in the doghouse!

We met a Welsh couple in another Bessacar. The usual red dragons all over the van! Stickers on the reg plate. Stickers on the windows. A big red rug on the floor and a cup of tea from a red mug! Not the slightest bit tacky!

"We're not English, honest" they moaned. What's all that about, eh? They're so scared of being mistaken for English. I love the Welsh but c'mon, we're all British and as no-one is about to move our little island to a different continent, we are all Europeans too!

~

We're wild camping in Peňiscola area this week. Love this place. It's our anniversary today. I better spoil her.

Best way to impress a lady?

Without a doubt, a candlelit dinner, a moonlit walk on the beach, and a seven hour medley of romantic, easy 3 chord guitar songs. You can't beat it.

Tip: Ignore my marital advice.

2023 Update – Seriously…ignore my marital advice!

Off further south next week.

Km walked 116. Pasties eaten 2. Beer guzzled (a lot).

Drew 200 Euros out of the ATM. Cost £199. OUCH!

I don't mind so much though. While I'm lying here at night I kind of feel a bit more sovereign, more British. I could never sleep before. Always felt like I had no control. Brussels was running my life. I'd wander round the shops aimlessly, worried sick about who was really pulling the strings in my life. Fifty six years of stressing.

I could never really see the point in working hard, starting a family, making a home etc...But now it's in our own hands. Now we can choose which jobs we want to do and which UK towns we want to live in. Most importantly now, WE can choose who we marry. We'll have no more interference from Brussels, unlimited cheap fuel and more tomatoes than we could ever eat!

Now that we're out of Europe and all those annoying Norwegians and Danish can't come over anymore, it'll be much better. They are a drain on our NHS (I reckon we should let the foreign doctors and nurses stay though).

I envy the youth of today. Imagine waking up in 2023 with the UK as your oyster, a properly funded NHS and millions of new jobs for white, British people. Anyway, we should've been picking our own fruit and veg and cleaning our own toilets!

Plus, the Pound shop can finally go back to being a pound shop!

☺

Chapter 10. Little bits of carrots

Over to Cataluňa. Weather is great here, though it's full of Catalans. Catalan flags flying everywhere. They're fighting in the streets. They want independence, apparently.

"Catalans, grow up. You're Spanish. You've been moaning since 1700. Get over it. You lost. Using your logic, I'm not English and I can be French because we had a French king in England back in 1216".

~

Tuesday 9am.

"Today, make sure you show me every photo of me before it goes in the book" the missus demanded.

"Eh, you what?" I thought. Jesus! I've taken over 1500 photos over the last few months but I've come up with a cunning plan.

"Bad hair day? A few spots? No problem. I have the solution!"

Strolling along the river in Castilla y Leon.

Posing above Miravet in Cataluña

Nice beach walk at Les Cases, Cataluña

She'll kill me for that! But who cares? It's my book!

~

Delta d'ebre.

Beautiful place to visit BUT Mozzies. So many that there is no airspace. You can see them circling, waiting for permission to land on your legs before biting you to death. The little b*stards! Millions of them all over the van windows!

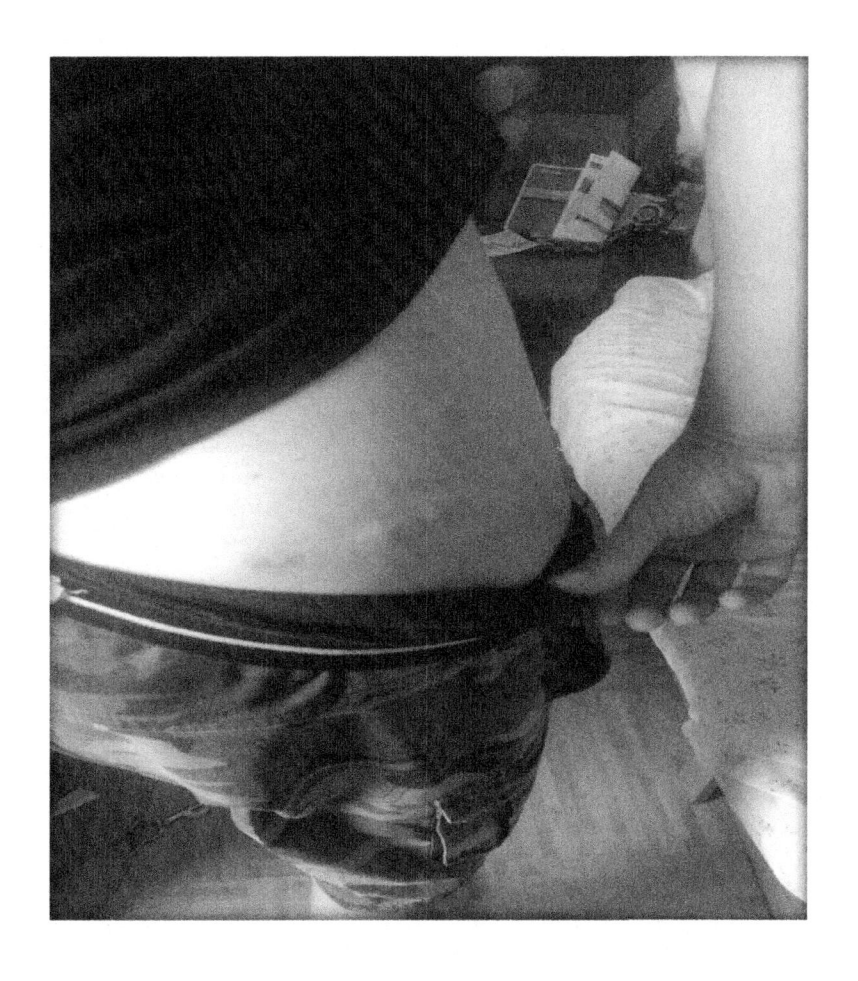

Delta d'ebre, don't go unless you swim in Deet first.

The missus is off to Mallorca to see her family again for a week. At last, some peace and quiet. Eat crap. Save all the dishes until an hour before she gets back. Have my breakfast cereal out of a pan. Watch boobs on the internet. I'll cope somehow!

~~SHIT~~ TO DO TODAY

DATE: _____ DONE ✓

1.
2. Tidy the van
3.
4. Wash all the dishes
5.
6. Wash clothes
7.
8. Wash the dog
9.
10.
11. Wash pits
12.
13. Trim my bits
14.
15. Pick up wife
16.
17.
18.
19.
20.

At Las Cases de Alcanar. Brilliant place to sleep, facing the sea. A few bars. Good restaurants. No bother from the police. Brilliant!

I'll go for a sneaky Indian while she's away. Tough! I deserve it. It's hard work all this doing nothing.

Halloween in Spain.

A time when children dress up in scary fancy dress and knock on doors asking for sweets. Aww.

Nope! Not in Spain. Halloween night is when 200 underage, Spanish teenagers get pissed off their heads on red wine & Coca Cola, blast terrible Spanish rap music from red Seat Ibizas, piss between your vans at 4am then have a nifty vomit next to your van tyres. Definitely not my favourite night!

The things women say.

The missus is back. Strolling along the beach, feet in the water, lovely sunny day when out of the blue she asks…

"What would you do now if you saw a missile coming towards you?"

"Pick up the dog and give him a last hug". I replied.

I'm on the sofa tonight!

In La Volta camping, Benicarlo, for a week. Cheap. Only 10 Euros with electric. Spotlessly clean. Highly recommended.

Chapter 11. I've got the wife an artificial leg

Our favorite place in El grau de Castellon has gone.
Se ha acabado. 'No motorhome' signs everywhere.

We were hoping to spend Christmas there so that's a bummer.

"I've got the wife an artificial leg for Christmas. It's not her main present just a stocking filler"

So, we're back parked facing the sea in Alcossebre. A place the police have told us to use in the past. No problem.

Relaxing one morning, reading the news online, when I could hear arguing outside in the street. Some old British woman was screaming at the Dutch couple in the van next to ours.

I opened the door, ready for action. She stares at me…

"Don't even think of raising your voice at me" I said.

"You can't camp here" she moaned.

"Camp? I'm parked actually" I replied. "I have the law here, in Spanish that states that it's perfectly legal to park here. Look"

"I don't understand Spanish" she muttered.

"And why not? I assume you're a resident here in Spain. Let's call the police then and wait here until they arrive" I responded.

"Sod off" she said and off she sodded.

She is a perfect example of what makes my blood boil.
A shrivelled up old, expat. Retires, moves to Spain then refuses to learn a word of the local language. She'd be quick enough to moan about the Indians or Pakistanis in the UK. Too thick to realise that SHE is an immigrant here.

"I pay my taxes" she screamed at me as she wobbled off down the street.

Well, that would have been 20 years ago and to a different country. You daft, old cow!

Shopping today. (The leaving the van check list)

Bag for life √
Dog √
Missus √

We went to the Supermercado for a few Xmas decorations for the van. Very clever people, the Spanish. For years they've been wondering how they can get more British customers into their stores. Then they sussed it. Put ' Supermarket' on the sign! Genius!

We're in the new motorhome aire for tonight. Storm coming, they say. It's hot. Every window's open. Lying there butt naked. Woke up at 4am. It was blowing a gale. Van rocking all over the place. I jumped up, climbed over the bed and ran round the van like an idiot closing all the windows before we lost one.

Next morning. 9am. "Christ, that was some storm, last night" she said.

"Yep, so bad you nearly moved" I replied.

I'm still coughing every night. It's been eight weeks now. Getting fed up. Doctors again tomorrow, I guess.
Update - Farengitis, apparently.

It'll soon be Christmas. Three more weeks until Morocco!

These winter nights are so long. Looking forward to getting stuck into some watercolour painting again. It's kind of my hobby. I've even sold a few ☺
Here's a couple of my efforts.

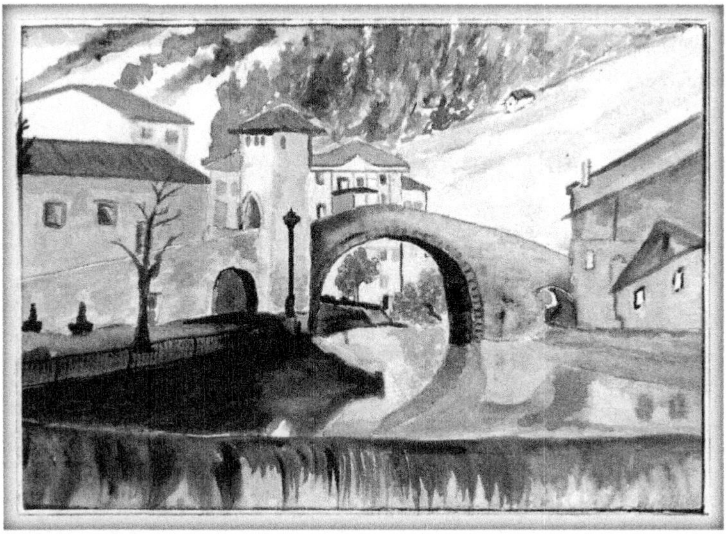

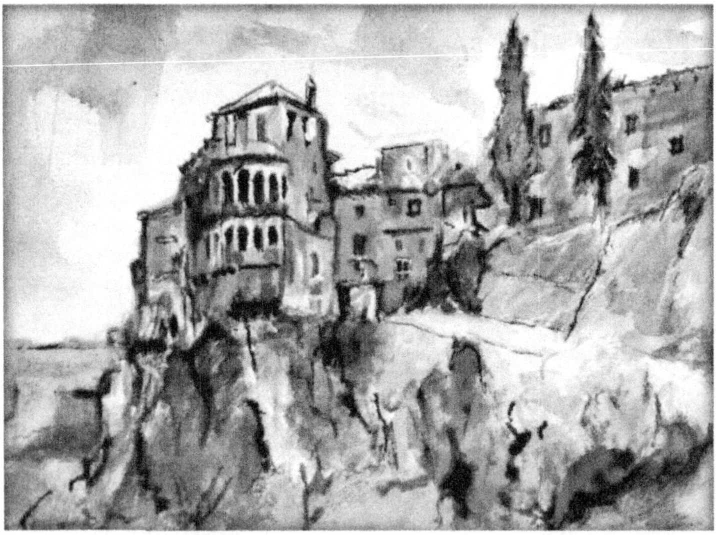

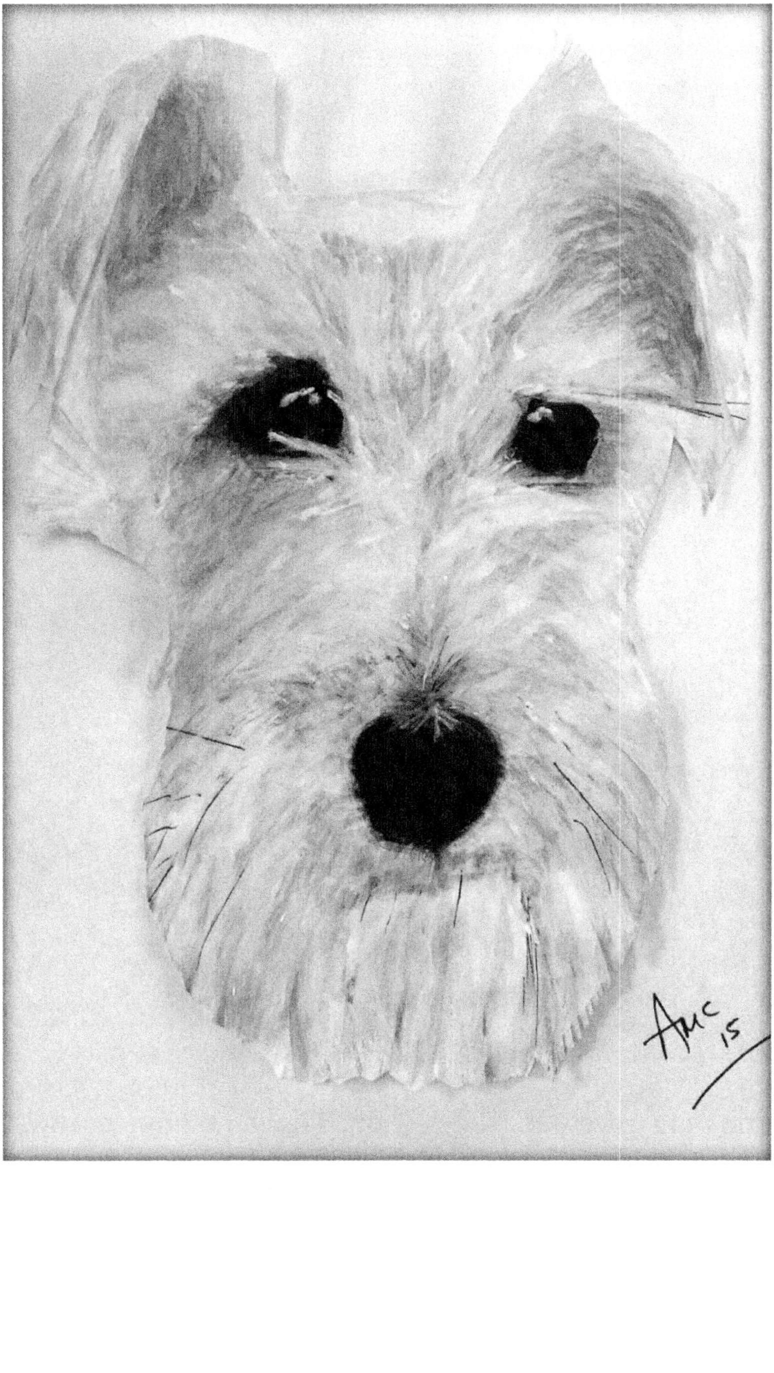
AMC
15

And lastly...Great Britain 2018. We've got ourselves a lovely, black immigrant princess, Meghan Markle. I nearly pissed myself. All those mixed race kids she's gonna plop out. Brilliant.

Mark my words. This won't end well. The UK press and the Gammons will hound them until they're gone from the Royal family. Little coffee coloured princes and princesses are just not going to happen. I'd bet my life on it.

2023 update – I told you so!

You may have guessed by now. I have no time for racists.

Kms walked 121. Pasties eaten 1. Beers quaffed 7.

Update : Since writing this book, Boris Johnson became Prime Minister of Great Britain, was an absolute disaster, repeatedly lied through his teeth and eventually resigned.

Good riddance!

An Eton degree is cool, but without a moral compass, you"re just a piece of sh*t – an educated piece of sh*t but still a piece of sh*t!

Chapter 12. "Eating on an empty stomach gets you pissed"

Storm's passed. Scooter off at last. 24° Razzed up through the orchards to Alcala de Xivert. Market Day. Full of the usual crap. The same market stall repeated ten times. Perfect if your shopping list is 3kg of oranges, a fake Levi's t-shirt, a pair of women's furry boots and some camouflage jogging bottoms. Still, it's amazing how many tangerines you can grab at 40mph! Freebies!!!

We moved back to the new free motorhome aire in Benicarlo and I whipped up a homemade, minced beef and onion pasty.

Just a little one!

Tip: Beware of the German nutter woman in the 2nd floor flat directly behind the motorhomes in Benicarlo. Put your step out and she'll be on the blower to the policia before you can say 'Heil Hitler'.

~

Shopping today for the Christmas dinner.

Yes, Southerners...it's called dinner and it's during the day. Not in the evening! Eg. School dinners, dinner ladies etc...NOT Christmas lunch! Just admit you're wrong, you posh gits.

Got an X-ray appointment in Benicarlo on Friday morning. Still coughing like a divvy. Fed up now ☹

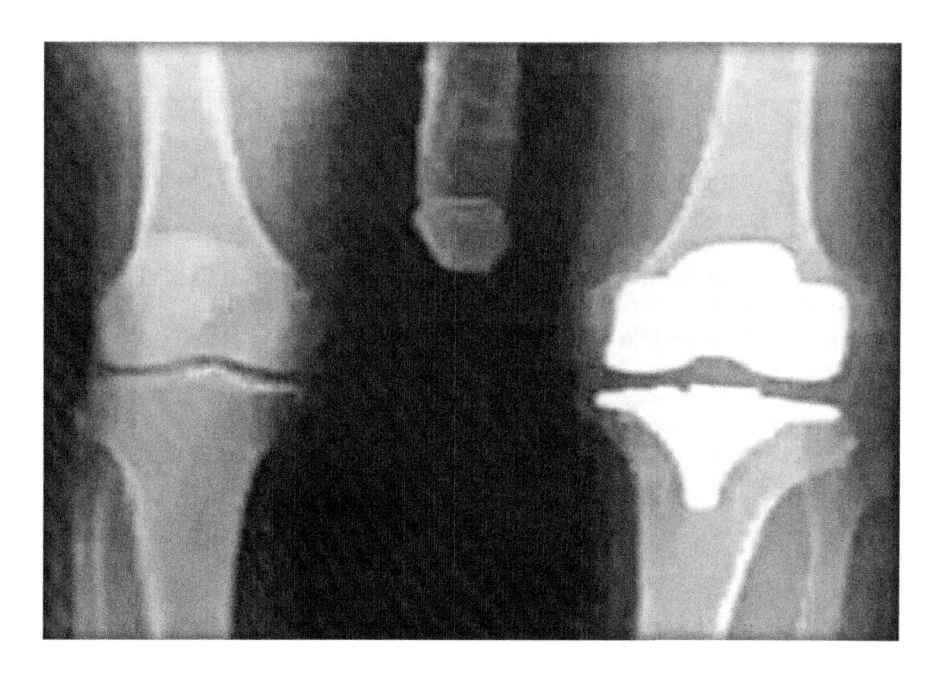

I don't know why they X-rayed my knees!

It's been ten weeks now, coughing. Kidneys are playing up too. Aching! I wish I had a twin. I could use him for parts.

~

Back to Alcossebre today, 30 mins down the coast.

I was giving tips about visiting Morocco to a couple on a motorhome forum and you wouldn't believe where they lived? Alcossebre. Just 100 yards away from where we were parked! What are the chances? Met up with them in RP's bar. Supped way too many vinos! Hungover now. ☹

The son's arriving on the train from Valencia for a few days, so we've gone into the new aire Las Moreras. Only eleven euros a night with electric and Wi-Fi. Nice place. New shower block and they're building a pool and bar for next summer. Biggest plus is that it's right in the center of Alcossebre. Plenty of bars, restaurants, shops and a lovely beachfront prom. Recommended.

2023 Update – They've completed the pool and bar. I can't recommend Las Moreras and the town of Alcossebre highly enough!

Christmas day tomorrow. New socks as usual, I bet. GREAT! YIPPEE!

Christmas dinner in the van. All day cooking, limited space, too many cooks and it's gone in 30 mins! Delicious but a lot of work.

"Two spuds! Are you having a laugh?"

Opened our presents. Got a little bit over excited! The missus accused me of being immature. I told her to get out of my fort!

The plan: down to Valencia on Friday, then Cartagena before crossing to Morocco next week. I can't wait!

Chapter 13. Where's all the camels like?

I love Morocco! We didn't really have a set plan but it definitely wasn't crossing just as a huge storm hit most of Spain and North Africa.

Nasty!

Voila!

It rained a lot for the first four days but it was just too large to outrun. They've said it'll be gone in a few days. Bought 20GB of Maroc Telecom data, so we'll watch a few films and kiss a bit, I guess.

Getting off the ferry at Tangier Med was an experience. They've built a nice new port with passport booths and everything BUT obviously, being Morocco, they never sit in them. It's like watching Man United's defence at Anfield. Everyone's running round like idiots. Chaos at its best. Great fun!

We stopped at Moulay Bouselham and treated ourselves to a campsite for a night. Just £7 with electric but the Mozzies in Moulay are massive. I mean MASSIVE. Be warned.

Shopping in Morocco.

If you've never been to Morocco before or you are the type of person that rapidly pumps antibacterial gel on your hands when a 'non-european' looks at you, then shopping for fresh produce here will give you a heart attack.

No nice neat trays of minced beef here. They chop it right from the cow as you wait. I think they are already dead though. At least, I didn't hear it moan!

Camel burgers for tea. Mmm!

Everyone here is so friendly and welcoming.

Ali, a Moroccan I hadn't set eyes on in two years ran up to me today in L'oualidia, all happy, smiling his head off and flashing his four teeth, just because he'd seen me again ☺

"Feesh, feesh, soul, crab" the fish traders scream. They take a bit of getting use to, the sellers from the port. Gordi keeps them away from the van, though. He hates them as much as I hate fish. He'd chew one, if he could get to them!

~

So, the missus woke up one day last week and she's like "Let's try this diet thingy everyone's doing. Mike with the hair says it's great"

Now, there are books that have been written throughout history that have caused a great deal of misery. A couple of examples being The Holy Bible and Alex Ferguson's autobiography.

But by far the worst literary crime against humanity has to be this 5:2 diet, fasting bollocks.

No more toast around the campfire. Crisps & wine, whatever! Chocolate, Doritos & two bottles of Rioja...stop dreaming!

I haven't had a sh*te in a week and my breath smells like a tramps kn*b! I've barely got the energy to write this page and I hate everyone!

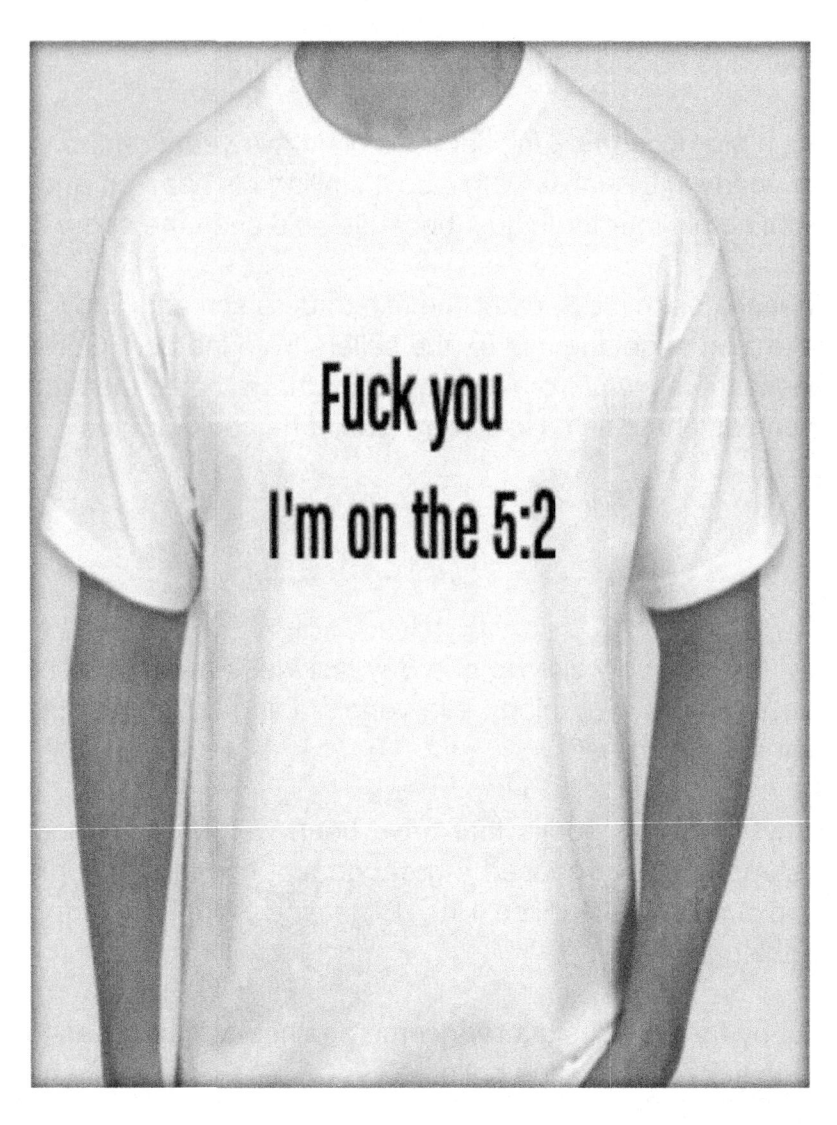

Try it. It's great! (or you could just try eating a bit less!)

The sun's out. Storm's passed. 24°. Morocco is great for the scooter.

Tomorrow, we're heading further south towards Essaouria. It's like a mini Marrakech but on the coast.
We love it there. Huge beach, plenty of restaurants and a great medina. Highly recommended.

Essaouira medina

Kms walked – Not enough.
Pasties eaten – 0. Beers swallowed – 10. (ish)

Chapter 14. Forks sellotaped to twigs

We've been in Morocco nearly a month. Loving it.

When walking up to the local kiosk thingy to buy some bottles of drinking water, a local man noticed that I was with three women.

"Pick the best one and leave me the other two" he said.

T'was a tough decision!

In L'oualidia, we passed a Berber woman, with wonky teeth. "Bonjour madame" she aimed at the missus. "Le pan, le pan, bread, bread" she screamed.

The next day, we offered her three times her asking price for a loaf and gave her a woolly hat. The guilt trip over. We'll sleep better tonight, I reckon!

We moved on to Sidi Kaoki, our favorite place up to now. Staying a week. So peaceful. Straight into the daily routine of getting water up from the well, collecting fire wood, making a fire pile and lighting it at 7pm. Brilliant!

Karen or 'Bacon Grylls' as we now call her is the best at water 'divining' and log hunting.

The bread delivery man comes every morning on his donkey. Only 15p a loaf. Hot buns too or maybe they're sweaty. Who knows? Who cares?

Pip with her sweaty bun!

Later, Veg man pops along. Only 5 dirham a kilo; about 40p.

We were shown a lovely place to park for a few nights, right on a deserted beach but as usual there was a price to pay; a pair of my old shoes, four fags from Pip and a drumstick lollipop!

Reality.

House problems and stress.

Monday, the oven in the house stopped working. New one ordered online. Electrician needed to install it. Tuesday, the tenant's in hospital. Annual gas check can't be done. Wednesday, boiler in house won't light. Plumber sent round. Today...some tiles moved on the roof during a storm and water poured into the bedroom. The tenants own £1700 mattress stained slightly. Argh!!!

~

Imsouane for a night then further south towards Agadir.

A little poem about Imsouane.

Maybe we'll go to Imsouane
Thinking of going to Imsouane?
Should anyone go to Imsouane?

No

It's time for a moan. I know this type of thing happens in most countries but when it happens to you at night when you are traveling with a couple of lady friends, well it kind of pissed me off.

We'd spent the day in Imsouane. Lovely walks along the coast above the town.

In the evening, we'd all walked into the port/restaurant area for a bite to eat. The electric was out in the town so we ate by candlelight, listening to a Moroccan drum group. Brilliant.

Okay, so we arrived back to our vans, legally parked in a public car park to find a soldier and another young Moroccan man banging on the vans.

"Eh you, STOP. What is the problem?" I asked.

"You cannot park here at night. It's dangerous. Not safe. Go to the campsite" the soldier said.

"So you are telling me that Imsouane is a dangerous place to park at night? Wait a moment. I'll get a pen and paper and you can write that down and sign it please" I said.

"No" he shouted. "Crazy black people are smashing van windows" he added.

"You obviously work for the campsite" I said to the young man accompanying the soldier.

"Yes, that is right" he said. "Leave this town or go into the campsite"

After wasting five minutes of our lives arguing, we left in the pitch black, slightly peeved.

We spend a lot of money in Morocco every winter. We love it but now not a single dirham of it will be spent in Imsouane. Ever!

We do use campsites when needed, but I refuse to be forced to by a corrupt soldier who's obviously taking a backhander for every van he forces into the campsite. Visit in the day, if you must but don't give that campsite your money.

Imsouane

Tomorrow, Agadir.

Chapter 15. This three wives idea is a nightmare

We passed through Agadir. Too European for us. A KFC, though! Spent the night on the outskirts then on to a little place just to the south of the city, called Tifnite.

Walking around nearby Tiznit, the next day, when a Moroccan came up to me. "I know you're English" he said. "You have food on your face...Is it Saffron?" "Err...No, its Spaghetti bolognaise" I replied.

We had been strolling through town for over an hour and not one of my 'three wives' had mentioned that half my dinner was still all over my face!

Thanks a lot ladies!

Fishy flip-flops. I love them. Stood in 'god knows what' in a Tiznit street. Flip flops needed to be soaked in a bucket for two hours and attacked with a hammer and chisel to remove what was stuck to the bottom!

Later, we parked up 15 mins west of Tiznit, on the front at Aglou beach for a few days. Under 2 quid a night. Nice place but it rained quite a bit. Never experienced that before in over eight visits to Morocco. Lots of barbershops here. Great timing. I've got a right bush head. I've been outvoted by the wives about getting myself a haircut. Three to one! Saved 2€ though, eh girls! Pizza money. Carrier bag on, clippers out. I'll do it myself!

At last, the weather has changed back to the norm for this time of year, 26°. Looks good for the week ahead too ☺

In Mirleft now, one of our favourite places in Morocco. It's Karen's birthday so we've decided to go out to eat. Ordered the usual, Beef & Veg tagine each, 2 big salads, 2 big plates of chips and water. £4 a head. Bargain.

Problem then is, you are left with 'Beefy teeth', all day and there's never a toothpick in sight. Then the 'Frites guilt' kicks in and we all have to do a four hour walk.

Gordi Baba in his element!

Corruption part 2.

In they charged again. 7pm. Half a dozen Moroccan soldiers in their, way too fancy, uniforms.

"You no sleep here. Forbidden" the sergeant shouted.

"For security reasons? I asked.

No answer.

"Tell me the official reason that we are being moved at 7pm, please" I asked again.

"Complaint from camping Erkounte" he said.

Well, there's a shock! A bleedin' campsite again!

What's ironic is that we were going to use that very same campsite in a few days to do our mountain of washing, fill up with water, empty the cassette etc...

Sorry Amir but now you've called your uncle Mohammed to move us, in the dark, I'd rather listen to Susan Boyles greatest hits than go into your campsite. Good plan Einstein. We'll give our money to the next campsite along, thank you very much!

PS. We'll be back here again tomorrow, parked in exactly the same place. So tough sh*t! You picked on the wrong fella, mate!

Chapter 16. Mohammed...2 pancakes in my gob, please

We stayed at Mirleft a bit longer than planned.

Lower temperatures up at Tafraoute, so we delayed going up for a few days. We've never experienced temperatures lower than 20° in all our years coming here so this takes some getting used to. Still drier than southern Spain though, this week ☺

A tiny van pulled up on the beach and out poured twelve young men. "Hello" they said. "Nice to meet you".

They told us they were students of the Quran. Lots of group photos then they climbed back in the van and left. A really friendly bunch ☺

The 2018 Take That Reunion

A few hours later, while strolling around the village, we spotted them sitting in a cafe. They called us over and next minute we were all eating gorgeous hot pancakes and drinking Moroccan (teeth rot) tea. Abdallah, their group leader is my Facebook friend now and the FBI have yet to raid my house!

Such a great experience talking to genuine, friendly people. This type of thing really points out what type of country the UK has become. Can you imagine a group of holidaying Moroccans being called into Sayers by a group of British to share their doughnuts and coffee. Not a chance! Correct me if I'm wrong but you know that it's true.

~

Up earlyish, before 9am anyway, and we're off to Tafraoute. The drive up was amazing although most of it was in 2nd gear behind an idiot in a lorry that liked to take every corner on the wrong side of the road. "Get out of the way, you kn*b". We finally arrived at the town and picked our spot amongst the palm trees that will be our home for the next month. This has got to be the best place we have ever found to stay in a motorhome!

Paradise.

It just doesn't get much better than this! Total peace and quiet. No-one moving you, plus perfect weather. What else could you ask for?

Home Sweet Home

We all rested for a day then we set off to the Lions face; an amazing natural rock formation resembling a lion. Over six hours later we arrived back at camp. Legs dropping off.

Slightly too much wood on the fire! Better get the fireproof trousers on!

Tip for Mike – If you're pissed, half naked & its 3am, don't start kissing dogs!

Serves him right for bringing that bloody 5:2 diet book!

The Surfboard hike above Tafraout. Knackered. Wobbly knees!

The Palm Tree salon opens at 9am

Tip : Don't keep your outside mat down with water bottles in Morocco. In less than 10 seconds the sun had burnt half a dozen holes in ours, like the laser scene from James Bond.

Kms walked - too many
Pasties eaten – 0
Beers drank - 38
Stress from renting out the house - Lots

Chapter 17. We love the French...Not

Stress from the tenants in the house. "Try paying your rent!" On top of all that, Gordi's turning ginger! Looks like we'll have to go home and sort it all out. (The tenant not the dog!)

It's over 36° today. Good day for walk, if you're a camel. We managed 24,000 steps. Way too hot. Siesta time!

I sold wine and beer to the local carpet seller. Sixty two euros. Over 42 euros profit. Cool! Then had a hair cut for 2.70€. The barber was a bit too touchy feely for my liking, though. Too much neck stroking, if you know what I mean!

Tafraoute is getting ready for the yearly Almond festival. Busy. Lots of stalls and a week of live music. The atmosphere is brilliant but it gets a bit too noisy to sleep. We'll do another night or two and then start heading back up north.

The painted rocks. Painted by some Belgian fella in the 80's.

Only a lovely, two hour stroll through the valley behind the vans. Perfect for the dogs.

Tip: Take a picnic and a lot of water!

Gordi loves Morocco. He runs around all day like a nutter!

Boo!

"It's a bit windy, like"

Climbed up to the top of the big pointy mountain. Made sure I wore my Liverpool shirt. It had to be done. **YNWA**.

The French.

What is it about the French?

Why do they think they can get away with being so rude? Last night we were playing cards in the girls van. A bit of sixties music on the tablet.

BANG...BANG...BANG. Someone was banging on the bonnet outside. So, I jumped out and some French idiot is waving his arms everywhere, like one of the Wright brothers!

He screamed something at me in French, which I assume meant 'turn the music down'

"Speak English" I screamed back, just to annoy him.

Now, I don't speak much French and he obviously didn't speak English but anyone normal with an ounce of manners would knock on the door if they had a complaint. What made him think that he had the right to bang on someone else's motorhome with his fists?

Firstly, we were INSIDE the van listening to the music on a 7inch Samsung tablet without a speaker. FFS.

Secondly, we are all wild camping. If he doesn't like something he can simply f*cking move somewhere else.

Morocco is great but the French ruin it, slightly.

"Listen, Pierre. Morocco is not French. It is not France. It hasn't been French for 60 years.

You are arrogant, eat weird food, make sh*t overrated wine and speak a ridiculous language."

(With heavy accent)

"We shall call 30, trente"
"40, we shall call quarante"
"60, soixante and 70 err.......err......err........sixty ten?"

What the f**k!

"Yes, then we can call 80, 4 times 20 and for 91 we can simply say 4 times 20 plus 11"

Superior race, my arse!

Heading north now.

Agadir.

Dodgy looking fella approached the van at the traffic lights. Automatically we think...'oh, oh, he's either after money or he's gonna sell me a goat'.

I wound down the window slowly and he offered me his hand to shake. "British. Welcome to Morocco" he said and off he went. Brilliant.

We're back at Paradise plage just south of Agadir, for our favourite Beef and Vegetable tagine. Only 2.25€. We went four days in a row. I could eat three of those a day! It's like eating a roast dinner without all the dishes plus Pip half-inched the left over bread. That saved us 4p!

"What do you mean you don't do bacon butties?"

A quick three hour drive up the coast and we arrived back in Essaouria. It really is a great place.

If you want to see it then take a look at the movie John Wick 3 (min 38). They used the city as Casablanca. It really is one of our favourite places in Morocco. So chilled!

Essaouira is one the highlights of our trip. It's famous for being Astapor in Game of Thrones and Jimi Hendrix spent time here during the 60's.

Walking along the new prom when a guy shouted over...

"English?".

"Yes" I replied.

"But you are laughing and smiling. You English are normally so serious and miserable. Are these your three wives? I love them. They look like Moroccan women, shaped like onions" he said.

No more pizza, cake and crisps for you, ladies!

While in Morocco we met a lovely family, Babiya, Zahra & little Adam. Babiya speaks French and Arabic, his wife Zahra speaks only the language of the Sahara and little Adam just smiles all the time!

Our new extended family!

We only said Bonjour and next minute we were having a feast in their house and dressing up in snazzy clothes.

'Rather snazzy'

Chapter 18. Spanish lesson for Brexiteers. Part 1

We stopped at El Jadida for a night. Had Moroccan soup out. Just 35p a bowl with fresh bread and it was delicious! Great town for shopping too!

Chefchaouen next. All blue. Brilliant for photos but not my cup of tea. Too busy. Nowhere to park. Too many tourists. Like a Moroccan Blackpool but less of a tacky sh*thole.

I'm exagerrating slightly, obviously. Chefchaouen is worth a visit. But there are just too many tourists for my liking.

"You can't sleep here" the guard moaned. Nightmare!

So, it's 6pm and we're off looking for somewhere to sleep before it gets dark. At 8.40pm we pulled up at a petrol station for the night. Nearly three hours driving in the dark!

Visit Chefchaouen, if you want but just for a few hours and leave while it's daylight. There is a campsite in the town but it's not the best and nearly always full.

The blue city

Chefchaouen

Why should you not kick an eight stone Alsatian whilst wearing flip flops?

A : It may turn around and eat you.
B : Your nail will fall off.

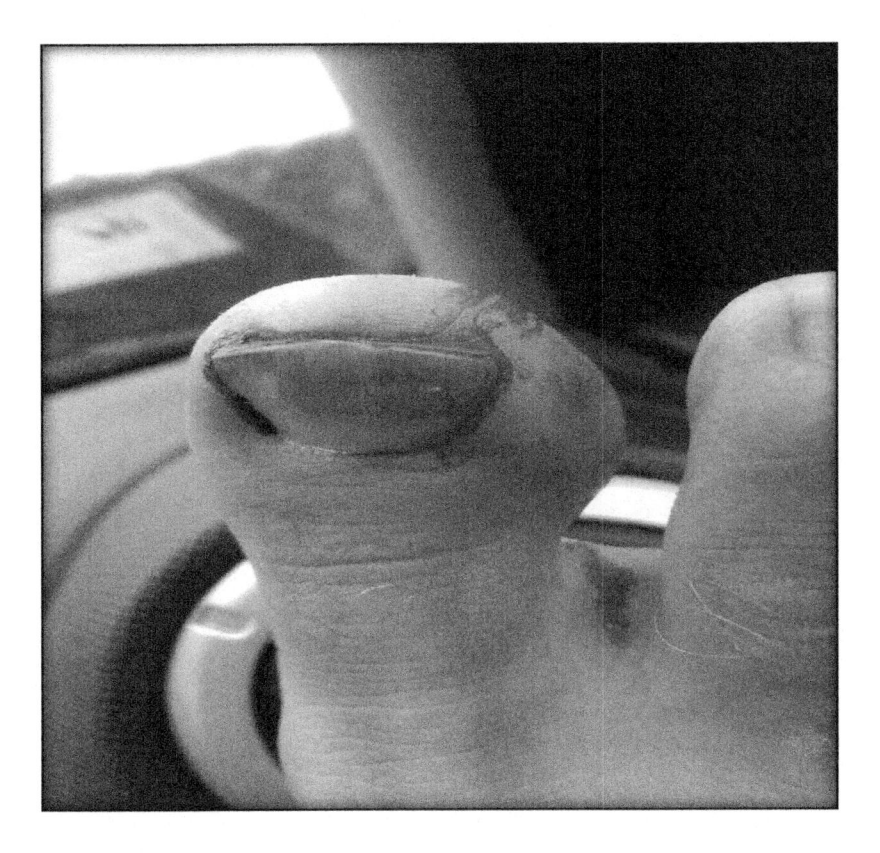

In Martil, the night before the ferry back to Spain, a huge Alsatian ran up and attacked our Gordi. That's the third time in three years, he's been attacked; twice in Spain and once here. Anyway, he fell ill. Bleeding from the arse and everything.

A visit to the vets, two injections, a week of tablets and a big bill for me and now he's fine ☺

I swear that the next big dog that is not on a lead and attacks our Gordi will get my hammer tapped ever so slightly on its head!

He's the best dog in the world, our Gordi baba!

Back to Spain tomorrow. We're sad to be leaving Morocco but our 90 days are up. Back to civilization. Catching the 6pm ferry back to Spain then planning on making our way east and up to Castellon before home.

Benalmadena, Torremolinos etc....

What can I say? The weather is nice but this isn't Spain.

Is it sunny? Yes, evidently it is sunny. Too hot in fact but don't worry ladies, Fat Kev will give you something to look forward to as you're strolling along Benalmadena prom.

He'll have his mate with him too, Big Baz. He'll be showing off his shit, faded football tattoo that he got after the 1999 FA cup final. He's got one in Mandarin too, on his belly. He's convinced it says 'Warrior' but it actually says 'Yogurt'.

"Let's go for a nice Cafe con leche on the prom", we thought. Over forty minutes later and we still hadn't found a Spanish cafeteria to stop at.

I don't want a 'Milky coffee and some Carrot cake' or a bleedin' 'Mug of tea with a teacake for 4,50€'. I just want a cafe con leche for around a euro. Should it be that difficult to find in Spain? Around here, yes! It makes me feel embarrassed to be British.

Having a coffee when I watched Fat Kev order "Two full English".

OK, I can help you out there, mate. I know it's difficult but with a few hours practice you'll soon get the hang of it.

The number 2 in Spanish is 'dos'.

So here we go..... "Dos full English, please"

See, almost fluent!

For years they've been moaning about the mosques in the UK and the foreigners being a drain on the NHS. Then they turn up in Spain, use the health service and expect everyone to speak English and serve British food!

"Rules and visas and all that crap should just be for them foreigners"

Learn some Spanish, you bone idle hypocrites!

Somehow, they can get their heads around their Sky TV box so they don't miss an episode of Emmerdale and they can work out how to stream the latest Tottenham match but then continue to spout "I'm too old to start learning a foreign language at my age"

BULLSH*T!

Spanish lesson for Brexiteers part 1

Learn these few simple words and phrases then you won't need them translating for you anymore.

Dentista - Tricky one this but if you remove the 'a' from the end you'll see a very familiar word.

Supermercado - I know it looks like Russian or Greek to you but if you look closely it's very similar to your own word supermarket. So if you see the word 'Supermercado', don't be scared. Go in. It's a shop.

Una pinta de San Miguel - Have a guess. Yes, it's a pint of San Miguel.

See, you're getting the hang of it now, Kev. So next time the waiter brings you your pint of lager you can say "Gracias" and NOT "Thanks mate"

Sunday opening and car boots in Spain. What's that about? Imposing your British customs on other countries.

Rooting around in a wheelie bin makes you a tramp.
Buying the same old sh*te off the floor for 15 centimos does NOT make you any less of a tramp.

Downloaded and watched Matt Damon's new movie, 'Downsizing'. Two hours of my life that I'll never get back. Thanks for that Matt, you turd.

More stress from the tenants. As you know, we are in the middle of a 12 month, once in a lifetime, non-stop journey around Europe and North Africa and now it's looking like we'll have to cancel it halfway through, due to what's going on with the house.

I'm angry but anyone that knows me well also knows that I'll have the last laugh!

Chapter 19. The tenants

It's pissing down in Castellon.

My kidneys are killing, so off to the docs. No appointment needed. Only ten minutes wait. Sorted! Two massive needles in the arse. Argh! I can't sit down.

Left Alcossebre to go to Pips Birthday party in Benicarlo.

Great night. Especially the bit when the owner of La Volta campsite wished Pip a happy Birthday over the mic. Cried with laughter. Could barely stand up. Big piss up!

"I wasn't there & we haven't touched a drop"

Lots of dancing and dressing up like The Village people!

Brilliant. I love Pip but she's crap at Fantasy Football!

Well actually, she's better than me but we can't let her know that, can we ☺

Back up to Fernando & Merche's in Cantabria for a few weeks while we sort out all the house problems then back to the trip. France, Italy, Germany, Czech, Holland and Belgium left to visit before October.

Looks like it's over. Nightmare. ☹ We might have to cancel the rest of the trip. The crappy tenants haven't paid the rent in five months. We're skint. Feel like kicking someone in the goollies. (The tenants)

The missus is back in the UK, yet again, so we can't meet back up with the girls yet. They're going on ahead without us. We'll meet up with them in Prague, hopefully. That's the plan but we'll see.

Lawyers. Doctors. Hospital. La Guardia Civil. Stress.
I'm downloading movies like a nutter. Tablet on the go, laptop on the go, mobile on the go. 138Gb already!!! (Don't tell Fernando or he'll turn off the router)

The missus is back and Fernando has finally decide to marry Merche. PARTY!

Here comes the bride!

2023 update – The tenants left eventually, leaving the house in a right mess but after threatening them with court, they paid all the rent they owed. ☺

Chapter 20. Icicles melt when you hold them

The French do 3 things well.

1, Cakes - Bloody gorgeous. I'm getting a fat arse.

2, Rain - It's always 2 minutes away from pouring down.

3, Err...Rain.

I tried to buy a decent pasty as we passed through Switzerland.

"What's dis?" I said in my best French accent. "You have anything wid pastry and meat?"

"Yes, It's a pastry with sausage, mustard and jam" she replied.

Really, I mean, really?

Stopped at Le Puy en Velay for the night. Impressive town. Highly recommended.

Free parking directly under the church on the big high rock. Apparently, they built the church there to be closer to god. I've always been told that he was everywhere?

The history of this church is hilarious.

According to the information on the wall outside, centuries ago a young girl decided to commit suicide, so she jumped from the top of the church. Just at that very moment the Archangel Michael was flying past and caught her before she hit the floor. Lucky eh. Phew!

Anyway, her mates didn't believe her so she jumped off again.

Go on. Guess what happened!

Yep, Archangel Michael was busy that day and she splattered on the floor. Hovis. Brown bread.

Since then millions of pilgrims have passed through the town on the way to Santiago de Compostela. Great for the town, eh. Not so good for the young girl.

A bit mean of old Michael the Archangel!

~

Up towards Alsace today.

The plan is to follow the famous wine route. A dozen lovely towns all in a row.

Internet with a UK 3 data sim is terrible. Too slow everywhere we've been in France.

I can't look at any boobs on the tablet. I suppose I'll have to look at the wife's!

A small deer ran in front of the van near the Swiss border. The missus was like "Aww". I was like "How would we cook that and have we got any mint"

Cernay. This statue really got to me.

A lot of people seem to have forgotten that we have had over 70 years of peace now in Europe. It should NEVER be taken for granted. I mean, look at the Ukraine!

During WW11 around 170,000 young French men from the Alsace region were illegally conscripted into the German army. "Fight for Germany or we'll deport your families to the camps"

Those that didn't die fighting were rounded up by the Russian red army and placed in labour camps and tortured. Over 70,000 of those young men died. Disgraceful. It must never happen again.

In Alsace now. What an amazing part of the world.

Colmar

I'll never moan about the price of a Sayer's pie again! 8.45€ for a beef pie & 4.95€ for a small one! So, I offered her a euro for a sniff!

Sorry, but I wouldn't pay that even if I'd won the lottery. It just wouldn't feel right. We just haven't got that type of money. I know where I went wrong. My Dad told me to invest my savings in bonds, so I bought 100 copies of Goldfinger.

We got the scooter off. Razzing around in between thunder storms. Riquewihr, Hunawihr and Ribeauville. Stunning villages.

Kayserberg is probably the most picturesque village that I've ever seen in my life.

I got a bit of grief on Facebook last month after sharing my post about passing through Lourdes. "What's that rubbish got to do with travelling?" some 'born again' genius asked.

Well, as I've said before, this book is about our travels through a Europe without borders before it becomes a lot more difficult as a Brit to do so. Obviously, being a travel related book, I will give my thoughts and opinions on places we visit and local food we eat etc...

So...we passed through a little town called Niedermorschwihr. The Virgin Mary appeared to a blacksmith in 1491 and told him to tell the people of the village to mend their ways and walk up the hill to pray for forgiveness. She was holding an icicle and asked him to lift up a sack of grain that she'd stuck to the floor, to prove his faith.

Now, for me, there are a few obvious, glaring errors in this story. Firstly, how did a 1st century Jewish woman from Galilea communicate with this 15th century French man?

Had she completed a Linguaphone course in the medieval French Occitan dialect or could she just speak every language on the planet?

Secondly, how did the Virgin Mary know about a tiny little town near the German border called Niedermorschwihr? I can't even pronounce it!

Lastly, icicles melt when you hold them!

> OK Google...
> Sinful French village?

All sounds fishy to me.

Anyway, now it's a big holy site with luxury spas and 5 star retreats etc, where you can repent and mend your ways whilst giving them all your money. Cool!

On the other hand, nearby Bergheim has a legend that over a thousand years ago villagers spotted a bear eating grapes. They tasted so delicious that they decided to grow them. Nowadays the region is a massive wine growing area and their 'mascot' is the bear. Which of the two stories above sounds more believable to you?

Walked into a restaurant in Ribeauville that was advertising breakfast 'at any time'. So I ordered toast during the French Revolution. No one laughed and they didn't even do toast!

With diesel being so cheap and the French roads nice and empty, I thought it'd be a good time to test out my theory.

The theory - If you do the exact opposite of what your Sat Nav tells you to, you will eventually end up in exactly the same place. So, if she says "take the next left", you turn right and if she says "at the roundabout take the first exit", you take the last. Genius!

Update. It doesn't work. I don't know where I am!

We loved France but glad to be leaving. What's up with the water? Really upsets my stomach. It goes right through me. In and out faster than a Daily Mail reader in a mosque!

Into Germany today. Parked up lakeside, just outside Triberg in the Black Forest region. So beautiful.

Triberg

Chapter 21. Propane is hard to light because of the dew.

Guess which country we are in?
All that's missing from the photo below is Steve McQueen.

This is more like it. Sun, at last! Get the factor 50 out!

Loving Germany so far. Cheaper than France and sunnier. Diesel 30c cheaper.

Lovely villages. Free motorhome aires. Leccy for a euro. Three euros a pint. We're following some of the Romantic road before heading east towards Nuremberg, Nordlingen. and Dinklesbuhl. Then over to Czech and back across Germany.

Currywurst? What's that about? Any idiot can cut up a boiled sausage and sprinkle some curry powder on top.

Pretzels? Don't get me started!

PLUS, THERE ARE NO PASTIES IN GERMANY!

Free motorhome parking in Harburg. We had a few big beers in Bamberg. Right facing the bridge. Great spot!

Next, Amberg. Yet another free motorhome aire. Electric, 1€ for twelve hours. I love Germany!

Can someone tell me where I can park a motorhome in the UK for free with services and electric for a quid. I'll compile a list on the back of a very small stamp!

In total we've spent only 4€ on parking in over 6 weeks of travelling around Europe.

I went off on the scooter looking for gas. I found it easy enough. Only 23€ from a really old German farmer.
"Do you have Butane, I asked him?" "Because sometimes, in the mornings, Propane is hard to light because of the dew"

Don't know why but he looked like he wanted to kill me!

Rothenburg. Jesus, was that a beautiful town. Visit!

Half of Japan were there, with their facemasks, as usual. No hayfever for them! (written pre-Covid, obviously)

Strolling around the town, I even saw electric hook ups for e-bikes. Guess. Free. Yes, FREE.

We were strolling around Amberg when I noticed that everyone was walking in and out of the shops with their dogs.

Eh...what's that about? I thought. So, I followed the missus into C&A instead of standing outside like a sad divvy for twenty minutes in 34°. It was like a zoo. I counted six dogs alone, just on the ground floor. Great!

No giraffes, though!

Kms walked 37. Pasties eaten 0. Beers guzzled 17.

The Czech Republic

Into The Czech Republic . We're going to see that church with the skeletons of 70,000 people in. Now, that's more like it! A bit of culture ☺

A striking resemblance!

The Czech Republic emerged from over 40 years of Communist rule in 1990 and joined the European Union in 2004. It's by far the cheapest place we've visited in the last 12 months (not including Morocco, obviously). Only 4€ for a pizza and a pint in Telc. Just 20p for a Marathon (Snickers).

Serious question though; Why is a Snickers plural and a Bounty isn't? Anyway, I love it here. Full of historic old towns and villages left over from the communist era.

So different to anywhere else we've been in Europe.

~

I've mastered the Czech language. I spent 3 hours per day for 2 months on Duolingo before we started the journey but in reality all we had to do was just add a Y on the end of every word.

I can't speak a word of it but eating out is so easy.

"We'd like 2 Steakys, 1 Burgery and a large Salaty, please." Done!

A bag of chippys and a sausage dinnery, please!

Down to Cesky Krumlov. Breathtaking village. One of the prettiest villages in europe. And just 60p to park overnight.

The UK could learn a thing or two from the Czech Republic. Free Wi-Fi, 220v sockets and USB connections. In the street! Yes, Free, obviously.

We're meeting up with the girlies in Prague today. Walked 20km. Legs killing! I'm getting too old for this. Too many tourists! Not as cheap as the rest of the country. Fancy buildings, though. One night was enough.

We visited Terezin detention camp, just north of Prague. Over 150,000 people were sent there by the Nazis. Nearly 10,000 of them were kids. Over 86,000 were later sent to Auschwitz to be 'exterminated'. The rest died of starvation and dysentery etc. Hardly any survivors. Really tough walking around reading their stories, seeing what they went through. Struggled and got a bit of wet eye ☹

This didn't happen in the Roman days or 1492. This is recent history. Generations of people systematically drip fed right-wing hatred by the media. Taught to believe that anyone different or foreign is a less valuable human being and is a drain on society. Sound familiar? Everyone needs to visit one of these camps. Especially now.

Day in Karlovy Vary.

For me it is the perfect city. Not too big, full of history and plenty of good places to eat or have a beer. So different to Prague. If visiting the Czech Republic, do not miss this city.

"I'm a lady"

We even managed to see Daniel Craig on the red carpet at the annual Film Festival!

Loket is gorgeous, too! So picturesque.

Only 1€ a pint and just 4€ to get in the torture chamber.
For an extra 3€ you can leave the wife there for a week.

I'd happily pay a lot more!

Next, Over to to Cheb to sit next to a lake for a few days.
Free parking and a nice medieval town to visit.

The beautiful market square in Cheb.

Back into Germany soon :)

Pasties eaten – 0 (don't exist).
Kms walked – A lot. 1€ pints drank – sh*t loads.

Chapter 22. Every woman should have a Titbag

Sat outside a Czech bar in Cheb with the girlies, Pipski & Kags.

Fifteen pints of Pils, 4 carafes of red wine (10 glasses) and 2 large bags of crisps. 24 quid! YES, 24 QUID.

That'd set you back at least £140 in the UK, I reckon.

Pipski staggered off to the loo and came back covered in blood! She'd fallen asleep mid wee and butted the metal toilet roll holder. As you do!

So, midnight comes and we're all linking arms doing the compulsory zig-zag walk back to the vans in the pitch black. Next minute we are all on the grass in a large screaming pile. Pipski's designer glasses lost forever. Never to be seen again!

So, bar bill = 24 quid plus 200 quid for new glasses.

They're dangerous, these cheap beers!

Finally got my medical results back from my Spanish 'finger up the bum' test. I'm hoping 'Negativo Crap' means I'm OK!

During the test, I took my trousers off and asked the doctor where I should put them. He said "Over there…next to mine". ☺

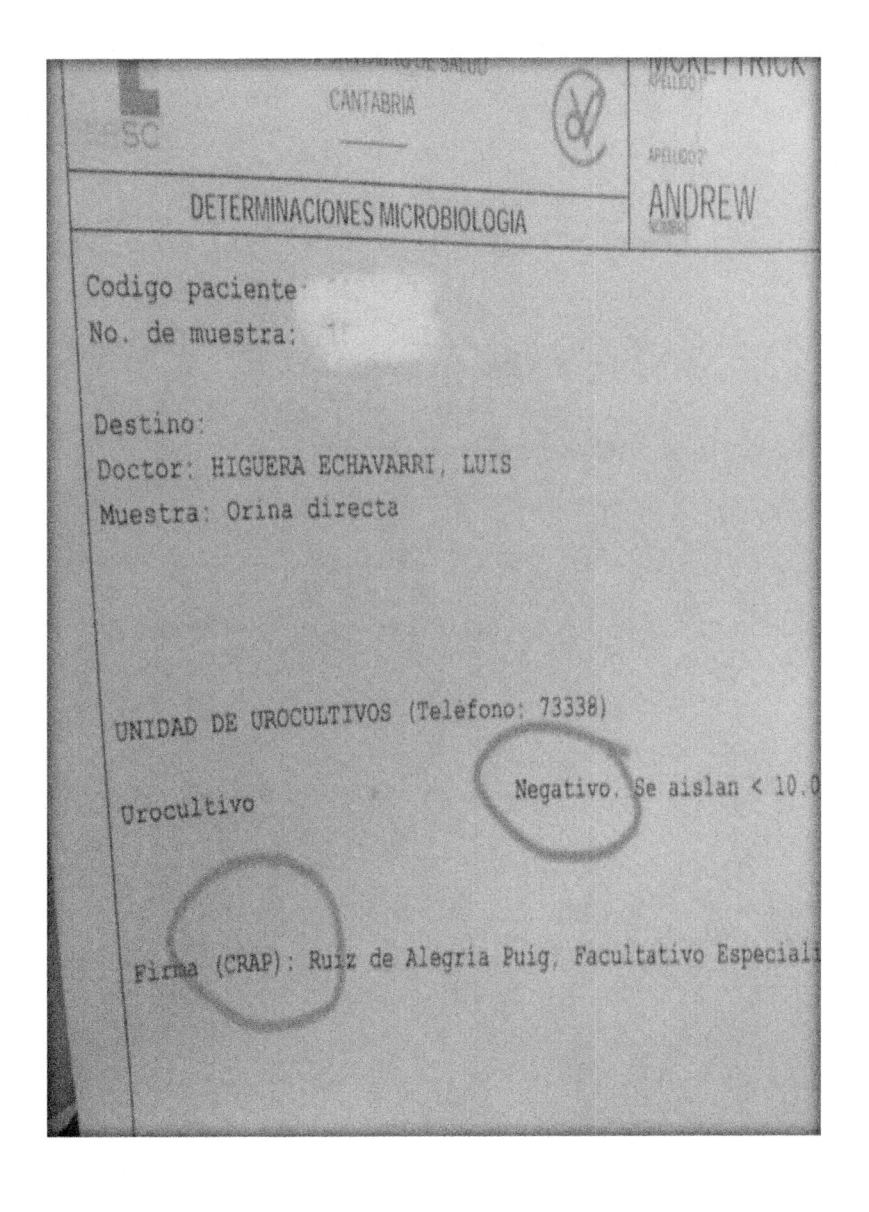

We found some interesting shops in the Czech Republic. This one seemingly does a nice bag for your tits.

Walked up the Big tower in Stribro. 592 steps. Who's bright idea was that? Not mine!

Next, on to Plzen, the home of Pilsner beer. Such a lovely, small historic centre. Recommended.

I had a haircut, we scoffed lunch in a Chinese restaurant, two cappuccinos and a 2 beers. Total spent between the two of us £13.50.   Wehe! My kind of city ☺

Back over to Germany today, land of free electricity and dodgy moustaches.

Chapter 23. Walking in Elvis's footsteps

We're back in Rothenburg. This time around, with the girls. Christ its hot! Around 36° at 9.30am. Too hot to walk and too hot to sit in the van. Dilemma.

I guess we'll walk a bit, have a beer. Walk a bit more, another beer!

It's the only way to survive ☺

Rothenburg. Such a beautiful village.

It seems that the whole of Germany decides to fix the roads in July & August.

Every single day we've had a diversion. Sat Nav keeps throwing a wobbler!   Tip = BUY A MAP.

The girls are heading for Holland before the crossing to the UK. Too far for us, so we've split up to head towards Luxembourg. I don't fancy doing an extra 700km miles to get to a beach. I think we'll stick to the rivers and lakes.

Stopped for the night at Wurzburg at the top of 'The Romantic Road'. Nothing special. Regensburg was much nicer. The Romantic Road spans 285 miles and takes you through historic charming towns and past some of the most scenic countryside in all of Bavaria. Definitely worth a visit!

Elvis Presley

I'd always wanted to see where Elvis lived during his time in the military. This was my chance. I've loved Elvis since I was a kid. Had the quiff and the suede shoes. I've fond memories of watching all the old Elvis films during Christmas week, every morning straight after Flash Gordon.

It felt great visiting all the places I knew he'd been.
First was Freidburg; Elvis was stationed there from '58 - '60.

Then Bad Nauheim - The house where he met Priscilla.

Me, walking in Elvis's footsteps on the set of G.I Blues

We thought Rothenburg was nice but the Marktplatz in Idstein is simply gorgeous. It's like you're in Disneyland but it's a real village!

We travelled west to the Rhein then along the Mosel to Trier. So much to see, including the Porta Nigra gate, the ruins of the Roman baths, the amphitheatre and the stone bridge over the Mosel.

We'll spend a few nights here, I reckon.

A German burger chain. Look at the name. I loffed my koch off!

This weekend, we parked up along the Mosel with a few other motorhomes, when a fella turned up in a Dacia and starts taking photos of our registration plates.

"Err...what do you think you're doing. Not without my permission" I said.

"You can't park here. I'm from the Bergermeister (town hall)" he replied.

"Then show me your ID please" I added.

"I haven't got any on me" he responded.

"So you work for the council and they send you out in your own car, wearing shorts, vest and flip-flops to take pictures of motorhomes? Give me your name, NOW" I screamed. He left in a rush, the fascist!

There's some really picturesque villages along the Mosel. Cochem and Bernkastel, to name a couple.

Along the Mosel

Crossed into Luxembourg today.

Only 1.10€ for diesel but that's about it, I'm afraid. Everything is so expensive. Over 9.50€ for a soup and 8€ for a bottle of beer. We miss the Czech Republic!

What's the point of Luxembourg? You've got to be rich to live there. They haven't even got a language. French, German, Luxembourgish...whatever. Take your pick!

You're never more than 30 minutes away from a cheaper, more beautiful country and there's only one nice town worth visiting. They don't even make pasties and even if they did, they'd be a friggin' tenner!

I've worked out why there are so many tree lined streets and leafy lanes in Luxembourg. The Germans liked to march in the shade!

Lidl here we come then back to Germany. A lot nicer!
I love Lidl. When I die, I want Lidl's bakery to do the catering for my funeral!

We've got a route sorted out back to the ferry. We'll do a bit more of Germany, into Holland, across Belgium then a little bit more of France then up to Dunkerque ☺

Our twelve month adventure will soon be over. I'm feeling a bit homesick. There's nowhere like Northern Spain in the summer. Normal temperatures, like 25°. I miss home.

Cantabria is such a beautiful place to live.

Home Sweet Home

(Available to rent, if anyone is interested)

It's just too hot here. Sitting in a seven metre plastic box in 33° heat at 11pm isn't much fun, plus I'm sick of sausages and beer. Well, I'm sick of sausages!

You know what I like about Germany, though? Their Jesus is rock hard. No messing around.

He'd be like...."Eh you, Roman. Do you like axes? Well, one step closer with that bleedin' crucifix and you'll be wearing this one". A Proper Jesus!

Next, Blankenheim then Bad Munstereifel. (Try saying that when you're pissed) Lovely places. Free parking, free Wi-Fi and medieval centres. Definitely worth a visit!

Into town for a birthday pint or two.

"Happy Birthday to me, Happy Birthday to me. Twenty one today, I'm twenty one today"

Whatever!

Kms walked 28. Pasties eaten 0. Beers supped 22.

Chapter 24. I thought I'd slip one out without you noticing

Last few weeks of our journey. Over 13,000 kilometres completed.

Monschau, Germany.

We've just voted it the prettiest village we've ever visited in our lives. Google it. It has everything, medieval centre, half-timbered houses and narrow cobbled streets but then again, all of Germany is gorgeous and brilliant for motorhomes.

In Monschau, I spotted a trendy looking Napflixen t-shirt. Only a couple of euros. Bought it. Thought it looked cool.

"Excuse me miss, can you tell me what Napflixen means please" I asked the assistant as I was leaving the store.

"Dog bowl" she replied.

"Dog bowl?"

"Yes, the container that a dog eats his food from. A dog bowl" she said.

FFS...Maybe, I won't be wearing it in Germany then!

I was leaving the shop when the assistant shouts **"Gute fahrt?"**

Now I don't mind the missus asking me that but a total stranger in public! What's that about?

I'm like "Yeh, it was actually. I had lentils for lunch. I thought I'd slip one out without you noticing". ☺

We visited Aachen, the closest German city to the UK then across into Holland.

We've seen some fancy buildings on our travels but the town hall in Aachen takes some beating and the Cathedral, Jesus! It makes the Sistine chapel look like a sh*thole.

I'm not really into churches but this one, you just have to see. If you only see one church in your life then make it this one!

Baarle - Nassau.

In this town the countries are all mixed up. People's houses are the Netherlands but their gardens in Belgium. The border even splits shops and houses down the middle. Weird!

Husband - "Have you seen the TV remote, love?"

Wife - "yeh, It's on the table in Holland babe and do me a favour, next time you come in can you please take your shoes off and leave them under the stairs in Belgium".

Back in France. No more Ice creams. No more beers. No more anything! We can't afford it. Germans are rich, no? So why does an ice cream cost 70 cents in Germany and 2.50€ in France? Thank god for Lidl.

Missus (looking at the map) - "Givet sounds like a nice place. Lots to see. Can we go there next?"

Me - "OK, we'll lock up and walk around it again after I've finished my sandwich, shall we?" ☺

We passed through Paris for the obligatory photo and a couple of six euro coffees, as you do!

Too big, too expensive, too busy and a nightmare to drive through in the motorhome!

Next we crossed into Belgium and stopped at the town of Dinant. Arrived around 5pm and it was pissing down. Parked up in the castle parking above the town. We couldn't find a way to walk down so let's ask the girl at the castle entrance, I thought.

"Excuse me, I said. How do we get down to the town?"
"This is the only way down, through the castle and it's €8.50 each", she replied

Disapointed, obviously, we walked back to the van, turned the chairs around, made something to eat and watched a movie.

The next morning we got up, had breakfast and then when leaving, the Sat Nav took us down the hill and straight through the town!!! Argh!

So, the 'Lying Person of the Month' award goes to 'The bird in Dinant castle'

Dinant

Sporting my new 'Dog Bowl' t-shirt.

Up to Tournai then Gent. The city of Gent is an amazing place. Like Brugge but a few less tourists. It's one of our favourite cities in Europe.

Beautiful Gent

I wasn't going to pass the Flanders region without visiting some of the WW1 memorials. We chose the 'Trench of death' at Diksmuide. Terrible, haunting place.

Both sets of soldiers spent years shooting at each other, only 50 yards apart. Can you imagine going through that? It makes you think. Maybe I'll stop moaning next time I get a splinter!

Christ, we have all been so lucky to have lived the last 80 years with peace in Europe.

Take a look back through the history of Europe. We have always been at war with someone.

Now we have 'men of the people' millionaires Farage and Johnson stirring up all this xenophobia. Funny how they always start moaning about people in dinghies right before elections to deflect from the real problems people face in the UK, like not being able to afford to heat your home or the highest rate of inflation since 1980. Maybe they could explain to everyone what they did with the 37 billion pounds they wasted on their failed Track and Trace app. That money would come in handy right now!

We're on the cross-channel ferry going to Dover and I can honestly say that I'm dreading the drive north.

Tip; Avoid eating on DFDS ferries. There's nothing like a delicious, Moroccan, vegetable tagine...and what I was given was NOTHING like a delicious, Moroccan, vegetable tagine! If you've ever wondered what became of Andrea Bocelli, then I can confirm that he's working as a chef on the 6pm crossing from Dunkirk to Dover!

"Ooh, Chickpea and vegetable tagine. That's better than the usual slop they serve on here" I thought, as I placed my order.

"Would you like chips or mash with that?" the lady asked. I should have realised at that point that something was amiss and changed my order to fish and chips!

Moroccan vegetable tagine minus the tagine & with chips!

Off the boat and argh...Straight into traffic. Non-stop traffic and mile after mile of cones. Also, a bit of tarmac on the M25 would be nice!

> 46
> ↰ Potholes ahead
> Remove dentures
> 1 km Fasten bra straps

Now as you know, we've travelled around a lot of European countries over the last 12 months and spent about £15 in total to park, in A YEAR!

We pulled over into a services a few hours after getting off the ferry at Dover and guess what? They want £35 to park overnight. Not £35 per year but per NIGHT! In a grotty service station, for christ's sake!

Question; why isn't it free to park?

Anyway, I hope you've enjoyed reading about our travels. It's been an adventure and I'd say to anyone contemplating doing such a trip, just do it. You only live once and life is short.

We visited 13 countries, spent quite a few bob in diesel and beer and loved every minute of it!

Our route over the last year or so

The journey is over now. We're back to a doing a fortnight here, a month there. It's a hard life!

Best place for motorhomes – Germany
Worst place for motorhomes – The UK
Most expensive places – Luxembourg/France/UK
Cheapest places – Morocco/Czech Republic
Friendliest place – Morocco
Safest place – Morocco
Best missus – Yet to be decided

Cheers and drive safely.

Andy

Ps...I've still got that sore inside my nostril. Over twelve months now. That Holy water from Lourdes is a scam. It doesn't work! Plus, we recently passed through France on the way to Mallorca and it was sunny. So, if you are going to France, I recommend August 23rd!

If you enjoyed this book and found it useful then I'd really appreciate it if you would leave a positive review on Amazon.

I do read all the reviews personally so that I can continually write what people want.

As if ☺

Chapter 25. Motorhome aires, campsites and places to park

St Omer 50.75665818, 2.259486

Montreuil sur Mer 50.75665818, 2.259486

Ville d'Eu 50.052827, 1.423376

Sanguinet 44.4855496, -1.08445840

St Savinien 45.833386, -0.646307

St Jean de Angely 45.945197, -0.537116

Souzay Champigny 47.241658, -0.022397

Bauge 47.539187, -0.096042

Candes St Martin 47.744799, -2.259895

Montreuil Bellay 47.131208, -0.160570

Vouvant 46.574604, -0.774722

Pouzauges 46.7761748, -0.8286108

Ste Suzanne 48.09935, 0.35043

Gaillac 43.894299, 1,897020

Castellnau de Montmiral 43.965801, 1.818630

Puycelsi 43.994400, 1.713740

Najac 44.221500, 1.967540

Lourdes 43.098301, -0.042208

St Jean Pie de port 43.165110, -1.231776

Ainoha 43.307164, -1.497526

Espelette 43.353500, -1.449610

San Sebastian 43.307896, -2.014580

Puentedey 42.977294, -3.683861

Cervera de Pisuerga 42.871537, -4.500113

Porto 39.5972235, -8.8207323

Vila Nova de Cerviera 41.937801, -8.747110

Ponte De Lima 41.767090. -8.591661

Guimarães 41.440784, -8.285998

Benicarlo 40.404099, 0.419943

Miravet 41.039727, 0.602782

Las Cases de Alcanar 40.552799, 0.529307

La Volta 40.398399, 0.402279

Alcossebre 40.245289, 0.271989

Moulay Bouselham 34.876112, -6.288480

L'oualidia 32.732171, -9.044122

Essaouria 31.530556, -9.689167

Sidi Kaoki 31.347908, -9.795129

Tiznit 29.714001, -9.710020

Aglou beach 29.804100, -9.827720

Mirleft 29.590232, -10.036768

Tafraoute 29.714957, -8.987450

Paradise plage 30.587681, -9.751177

El Jadida 33.249224, -8.450520

Chefchaouen 35.175500, -5.266760

Benalmadena 36.593370, -4.531507

Le Puy en Velay 45.044715, 3.894911

Cernay 47.802883, 7.167845

Colmar 48.080502, 7.373490

Riquewihr 48.166100, 7.301540

Hunawihr 48.179081, 7.312073

Ribeauville 48.190788, 7.329610

Kayserberg 48.136200, 7.261930

Triberg 48.132323, 8.232549

Harburg 48.785702, 10.691300

Amberg 49.428207, 11.853648

Rothenburg 49.386230, 10.155820

Prague 50.061634, 14.413923

Cesky Krumlov 48.818711, 14.266447

Terezin 50.511403, 14.150129

Karlovy Vary 50.212769, 12.888085

Loket 50.188801, 12.750600

Cheb 50.090945, 12.281907

Plzen 49.790942, 13.168644

Regensburg 48.927299, 12.040500

Freidburg 48.015929, 7.834160

Bad Nauheim 50.368245, 8.731350

Idstein 50.226694, 8.226244

Trier 49.739540, 6.648441

Cochem 50.153537, 7.168209

Bernkastel 49.918945, 7.059712

Puente Viesgo 43.296285, -3.965018

Blankenheim 50.442690, 6.592774

Bad Munstereifel 50.553610, 6.758996

Monschau 50.544435, 6.285950

Aachen 50.770109, 6.048434

Baarle – Nassau 51.440781, 4.931483

Givet 50.143200, 4.826170

Dinant 50.267101, 4.934540

Tournai 50.604099, 3.380820

Gent 51.037201, 3.767090

Diksmuide 51.033760, 2.762529

Note – Many of the towns and villages above have various places to park overnight. I recommend using the great apps Park4night and Searchforsites when deciding where to stay.

Galicia - Northern Spain

The Anti-Atlas - Morocco

Our Baba

El Churron de Borleña, Cantabria

Anfield - Where it all began!

Beachy Head UK

Tafraoute – Morocco

Potes – Northern Spain

L'Oualidia – Northern Morocco

I've come to the conclusion that vanlife is no good for your looks!

Inside the city walls - Essaouira

Baba in Montreuil Sur Mer

Brighton beach

Somewhere in Morocco!

The BIGGEST MISTAKE
We Make In LIFE
Is Thinking
WE HAVE TIME